JUDGING INEQUALITY

53
Leo

The Cobden Trust

The Cobden Trust is a registered charity established in 1963 to seek the protection and extension of civil liberties in the United Kingdom by researching the causes of injustice and educating the public about their rights and responsibilities.

How you can help

While we are able to raise funds from charitable trusts and foundations, we depend also on generous public support. As a registered charity, the Trust can recover tax from the Inland Revenue on any covenanted donation. If you would like to help us in this way, or would like further information, then please write for details to the Secretary, the Cobden Trust, 21 Tabard Street, London SE1 4LA.

JUDGING INEQUALITY

*The Effectiveness of the Tribunal System
in Sex Discrimination and Equal Pay Cases*

Alice M. Leonard

The Cobden Trust

The Cobden Trust
21 Tabard Street
London SE1 4LA

ISBN 0 900137 28 2

© Alice Leonard 1987

British Library Cataloguing in Publication Data

Leonard, Alice M.
    Judging inequality: the effectiveness of the tribunal system in
sex discrimination and equal pay cases.
    1. Sex discrimination against women – Law and legislation –
Great Britain
    2. Sex discrimination in employment – Law and legislation –
Great Britain
    I. Title
    344.104'14   KD3103.W6

    ISBN 0-900137-28-2

Typeset, printed and bound in Great Britain by
The Yale Press Limited, London SE25 5LY

For my parents

ACKNOWLEDGEMENTS

I am very grateful to the German Marshall Fund of the United States and to the Nuffield Foundation, who provided the funding for this research; and to the London School of Economics and the University of Bath, who made their facilities available to me. I would also like to thank both the Equal Opportunities Commission and the Central Office of Industrial Tribunals, who provided assistance on numerous occasions. Many individuals helped in many ways, but I would particularly like to thank Jennifer Corcoran, Elaine Donnelly, Bob Hepple, Sara Huey, Christine Jackson, Colin Lawson, Paddy Stamp and Michael Zander.

CONTENTS

FOREWORD

This timely and important study deserves to be read by everyone interested in the enforcement of anti-discrimination legislation, and by those concerned with the operation of industrial tribunals.

It is timely because of the current debate about the ways in which the Sex Discrimination and Equal Pay Acts – in force for more than a decade – could be improved. The Equal Opportunities Commission published a consultative document late in 1986, "Legislating for Change". Many organisations and individuals have already put forward ideas. In the closely related field of racial discrimination the Commission for Racial Equality published its proposals for reform in 1985.

It is important because it is the first detailed empirical study of tribunal hearings and decisions in sex discrimination and equal pay cases. It enables us to test the views of critics and defenders of the system against a comprehensive review, instead of relying on partial and anecdotal evidence. Alice Leonard has brought to this investigation her skills as a lawyer with extensive practical experience of handling civil rights cases in the United States, the country whose laws were the model for much of the Sex Discrimination and Race Relations Acts. She has analysed all tribunal decisions relating to sex discrimination and equal pay over a three-year period (1980-82). In addition, she observed a number of hearings and interviewed participants in the system.

Her findings (summarised in Chapter 6) are disturbing. The tribunal decisions reveal ignorance and misunderstanding about the Acts. Many tribunals applied the wrong legal standard, confusing the test for direct discrimination ('less favourable treatment') with the more familiar test for unfair dismissal (the range of responses of the 'reasonable' employer). Despite the Employment Appeal Tribunal's guidance that the tribunals should require a 'clear, specific and credible' explanation, other than the reason of sex, for discriminatory treatment, tribunals were found to be superficial in their analysis of the evidence, too ready to accept vague and generalised statements even where these appeared to be inconsistent with other evidence, or based on irrelevant considerations such as 'benevolent' motives.

The lack of uniformity in the approach taken by different tribunals, which Alice Leonard explains as being related to the level of expertise of the complainant's representative as well as to the expertise of the particular tribunal panel, has doubtless been exacerbated since the period of this study by the recent tendency of the Court of Apeal and the Employment Appeal Tribunal to categorise crucial issues, such as the 'justifiability' of indirect discrimination, as questions of 'fact' for the tribunal. This means that tribunals are expected, by a process of fact evaluation, to decide on the comparative importance of eliminating discriminatory practices on the one hand, as against, for example, the profitability of a business on the other. This is an area in which no consensus exists among tribunal members, even less a social consensus. Not surprisingly, therefore, tribunals increasingly tend to reach inconsistent decisions.

Alice Leonard pinpoints the lack of training and lack of opportunity to develop expertise as factors responsible for the relatively poor performance of tribunals. Sex and race discrimination cases constitute less than 3 per cent of the tribunals' caseload and the policy of random distribution of cases has meant that few chairmen and lay members have been able to become expert in this, the most complex of all the tribunals' jurisdictions. Some of Alice Leonard's recommendations, for example for the presence of full-time rather than part-time chairmen, are now usually followed in practice. Several regions are also adopting a case assignment procedure which develops expertise in at least a few chairmen and panel members, but there still appears to be no national policy of specialisation in England.

Perhaps the most important of Alice Leonard's findings is that most claims do not succeed because of the failure by complainants and their representatives to present to the tribunal relevant evidence sufficient to support their claims. The study reveals that the usual pattern is for the parties to present only oral testimony, with no more than one or two pre-existing documents; they neglect to call supporting witnesses, fail to cross-examine effectively, and make little or no use of statistical and comparative evidence. Not surprisingly, she shows that the success rate of claims rose directly with the amount of documentation available to the tribunal, and that complainants with legal representatives, particularly those knowledgeable and experienced in equal rights legislation, were more likely to succeed.

Many of Alice Leonard's recommendations, such as ways of improving legal advice and representation, will command widespread support. She also identifies a number of more controversial proposals: Should the burden of proof be changed? Should there be a special 'discrimination division' in the ·tribunals? Should a form of class action be introduced? Should the adversarial model be modified?

Whatever conclusions the policy-makers reach on these and other issues, we must all be thankful to Alice Leonard for undertaking this extremely thorough and illuminating study of how the system actually works, and to the Cobden Trust for publishing it.

BOB HEPPLE*

1 September 1986

* Professor of English Law in the University of London at University College; Chairman of Industrial Tribunals (England and Wales); member of the Commission for Racial Equality.

ABBREVIATIONS

ACAS	Advisory Conciliation and Arbitration Service
CAB	Citizens' Advice Bureaux
COIT	Central Office of Industrial Tribunals
CRE	Commission for Racial Equality
EAT	Employment Appeals Tribunal
EOC	Equal Opportunities Commission
EQPA	Equal Pay Act
DE	Department of Employment
ICR	Industrial Court Reports
IRLR	Industrial Relations Law Reports
NCCL	National Council for Civil Liberties
ROIT	Regional Office of Industrial Tribunals
SDA	Sex Discrimination Act

INTRODUCTION

The Sex Discrimination Act 1975 (SDA 1975) and the Equal Pay Act 1970 (EQPA 1970), as amended by the 1975 Act, provided a comprehensive statutory scheme prohibiting discrimination on the grounds of an individual's sex, in all aspects of employment, i.e. recruitment, training, promotion, benefits, pay and dismissal, as well as in education, housing, and the provision of goods, facilities and services. The SDA 1975 also established the Equal Opportunities Commission (EOC) and gave it a mandate to encourage the elimination of discrimination, promote equality of opportunity between men and women and monitor the effects of the two Acts themselves. Yet unlike two other anti-discrimination enforcement agencies – the Race Relations Board (which preceded it) and the American Equal Employment Opportunities Commission (which in other respects it greatly resembles[1]) – the EOC was *not* given the responsibility for receiving and investigating complaints of discrimination from individuals. Instead, individuals with complaints of discrimination in any aspect of employment[2] were given the right of direct access to industrial tribunals: informal judicial bodies entirely independent of the EOC, which adjudicate various other employment-related claims.

The decision to give individuals the right of direct access to the tribunals was deliberate. In part, it was the result of dissatisfaction with the scheme provided under the Race Relations Act 1968, whereby individuals' complaints were subject first to conciliation by the Race Relations Board and, if conciliation failed, the Board had the sole power to initiate civil legal proceedings. Under the new scheme individuals benefitted, at least in theory, from greater control over their own complaints, which they could file with the tribunals without procedural delays. In addition, it was felt that the EOC would benefit from this innovation in several respects. As the EOC itself has explained:

> An . . . important weakness of previous legislation was that, to the extent that it relied upon spontaneous complaints from individuals, the priorities of the [Race Relations] Board were determined by whatever happened to be the pattern of complaints that had been lodged. It was not required to take an independent initiative through its own investigation of the true pattern of discrimination, even though its experience suggested that reliance upon complaints both understated the extent of discrimination and misrepresented its true

incidence. The procedure established by the Sex Discrimination Act placed upon individuals the principal responsibility for seeking redress before industrial tribunals and county courts. The Commission was thus freed to concentrate on the important strategic role of seeking out patterns of discrimination and bringing the law to bear upon them.[3]

The additional reason given for freeing the EOC from holding exclusive responsibility for individual complaints was a practical one: the Race Relations Board's experience had indicated that any such agency would be so occupied dealing with individual complaints, that it would not have the time or resources to properly fulfil the positive independent role originally envisaged by the two parliamentary select committees.[4] The EOC nevertheless has discretion to provide individuals with assistance ranging from advice to legal representation in the industrial tribunals and the courts. It can provide legal assistance in cases which raise important legal issues, matters of principle, or have special importance for some other reason. However, it has generally remained committed to maintaining primary emphasis upon its strategic role, looking to the industrial tribunals as the primary vehicle for the resolution of individual complaints of sex discrimination in employment.

The industrial tribunals were created by the Industrial Training Act 1964 to deal with appeals against certain industrial training levies authorised by that Act. The tribunals' jurisdiction has since been extended to several additional areas, including the scheme of redundancy payments under the Redundancy Payments Act 1965, claims of unfair dismissal created by the Industrial Relations Act 1971, and claims of race and sex discrimination in employment, in addition to some other esoteric areas.[5] From an initial caseload of several hundred, they now receive some 40,000 complaints each year, approximately two-thirds of these ending in withdrawals or negotiated settlements and therefore not requiring a tribunal hearing.[6]

When the tribunals were first established they were envisioned as a fair and efficient way of adjudicating individual claims relating to employment and, as such, they were thought to offer several advantages to claimants under the sex discrimination and equal pay legislation. The speed and low cost of the system were expected to encourage men and women to seek redress of discriminatory acts against them. The participation of lay members with backgrounds in trades unions and management was believed to provide valuable expertise in considering issues related to employment. The system was certain to avoid repeating the American experience where individuals find themselves waiting years for judicial resolution of their discrimination claims. Moreoover, there were undoubted advantages in using an established system to process claims under what could be considered 'radical' legislation. There were some complaints that the tribunals were not the best forum for deciding equal rights claims and even clear opposition from some quarters[7] but, on balance, the system appeared to offer certain important advantages.

In the years since the enactment of the equality legislation, however, there have been indications that applicants are encountering problems in pursuing sex discrimination and equal pay claims through the tribunals. The success rate of applications seems quite low: of 1,794 sex discrimination claims and 4,296 equal pay claims filed from 1976-1983, fewer than 11% were successfully concluded after a tribunal hearing.[8] The numbers of applications to the tribunals have declined drastically from those in the early years.[9] Research on the performance of the Advisory, Conciliation and Arbitration Service (ACAS), the body which assists complainants to tribunals to reach negotiated settlements with their employers, has identified problems which are also likely to be encountered by those who continue to tribunal hearings.[10]

Criticism has been voiced by barristers and solicitors who handle sex discrimination claims, by advocates and academic commentators, and even by several tribunal chairmen who have stated that, in various respects and for various reasons, the tribunal system as it currently operates is not conducive to the proper development and presentation of the legal and factual issues in sex discrimination and equal pay cases, since these are often complex and/or novel. For example, several academic and practising lawyers have written about the legal complexities and difficulties of the legislation, the problems of obtaining evidence of discrimination, the burden of proof and the inadequacy of the tribunals' remedial powers.[11] There has also been criticism of tribunal panels, both of chairmen and lay members.[12] In short, there are several important reasons to question whether the tribunal system is actually providing equal rights complainants with the accessible, informal, and expert adjudication of claims initially expected.

To date, however, there has been no empirical analysis of the way in which the system is handling sex discrimination and equal pay claims: no thorough examination of the way in which cases are developed, presented, and decided. In fact, virtually no information has been developed about the types of complaints filed, the parties, the chairmen and panel members who were hearing the cases, the evidence presented at hearings, or the tribunals' patterns in reaching decisions.[13] Nor has there been any attempt to

3

determine what circumstances contribute to the success or failure of complainants at tribunals. So although there is anecdotal evidence of problems and commentators have expressed opinions about what they are and what might solve them, it has not been possible to test their opinions against empirical evidence, nor to predict whether changes which they propose are actually likely to succeed.

A principal objective of this study was therefore to develop as thorough and accurate a factual description as possible of the development, presentation, and adjudication of sex discrimination and equal pay claims in the industrial tribunals. This approach serves two distinct purposes. First, it identifies problems that exist and possible ways of minimising or eliminating them. Secondly, it provides evidence to test the criticisms of the system, and to illuminate the debates about and the proposals for change which have been made by other commentators.

The study was undertaken in 1983-1984. It focuses specifically upon tribunal hearings on sex discrimination and equal pay claims although, in gathering information about these and in interviewing participants and others, the inquiry inevitably ranged more widely. However, the issue of the conciliation process and the question of the actual enforcement of decisions were excluded; the former being the subject of a major investigation elsewhere[14] and the latter having been examined subsequently in a separate study.[15] No doubt, some of the observations made or conclusions drawn in this study will also hold true for other types of claims heard by the tribunals, the most probable being those of racial discrimination in employment and, possibly, claims of unfair dismissal, which constitute the largest proportion of the tribunals' work. At the time this study began, however, separate major research efforts were underway in both of those areas,[16] and so they were also excluded from consideration. There were four sources of information:

Tribunal hearings. Hearings on sex discrimination and equal pay claims were observed in each of the several regions in the southeast and southwest of England, and in the Midlands (London, Ashford, Exeter, Bristol, Birmingham), and in Scotland. The hearings which were observed in 1983 and 1984 were selected to include a range of issues, different types of representation and both female and male complainants; notification of the hearings scheduled having kindly been supplied by the offices of the Presidents of the Industrial Tribunals for England and Wales, and Scotland. The complainant, respondent, their witnesses and their representatives were interviewed after each hearing and, except in one region, matters such as case scheduling and the assignment of chairmen and panel members were discussed with tribunal administrative staff.

Tribunal decisions. In order to obtain a wider picture, the study undertook a detailed analysis of all tribunal decisions relating to sex discrimination and equal pay applications issued by the tribunals between 1 January 1980 and 31 December 1982.[17] During this three-year period, a total of 298 decisions were issued in England, Wales and Scotland. Of these, special attention was given to the 227 decisions on the full merits, which provided information about the complainant(s), respondent(s), type of claim(s), tribunal chairmen and panel members, evidence and witnesses presented, length of hearing, parties' representation, various aspects of the tribunal's analysis and findings and the outcome of the case. (Of these 227 decisions, 215 were from England and Wales and 12 from Scotland.)

Interviews. Ten tribunal chairmen were interviewed in the course of the study, most of whom had a particular interest in sex discrimination and equal pay claims. These were in addition to those chairmen observed at hearings. Interviews were also conducted with tribunal members other than those observed at hearings; barristers and solicitors experienced in representing complainants in equal rights cases; individuals at the EOC, the EOC of Northern Ireland, NCCL Women's Rights Unit; and academics in law, industrial relations and politics at the London School of Economics, University College (London), the (then) Economic and Social Science Research Council's Industrial Relations Unit at the University of Warwick, and the University of Bath.

Statistics on representation. These were kindly provided by the Department of Employment (DE) and the Central Office of Industrial Tribunals (COIT).

Information from the case decisions served as a basis for observations about the way cases are presented to the tribunals and decided by them, and as the data source for statistical analyses of the effects of different factors on case outcome. The observations at hearings and the interviews served to suggest lines of inquiry and to confirm or modify conclusions drawn from case decisions.

This study aims to determine how the tribunal system is applying the SDA 1975 and EQPA 1970 as they are currently written and interpreted. It is not directly concerned with questions of scope and therefore does not address the issue of whether the Acts or any of their particular provisions are, in themselves, too broad or too restricted. In part this is because the inadequacies of the Acts are by now well-known, or at least the subject of debate.[18] Mainly, however, this is because even a 'perfect' statute is effective only if it is correctly applied and enforced. Changes in a statute – whether substantial or mere tinkering – will have little impact if the system by which they are applied is uninformed or for other reasons inadequate for the job. The objective of this study is therefore to determine how the tribunals are performing their task, the reasons for any apparent failures and the possibilities for improvement.

Chapter 1 provides a brief outline of the procedure for filing a claim of sex discrimination in employment or for equal pay and the manner in which such claims proceed to a final tribunal hearing. The second part of the chapter contains basic descriptive information developed on those sex discrimination and equal pay claims decided by the tribunals during the period studied: the types of claims, the complainants (their sex, occupation, number per case), the respondents (their type of business, size of workforce); it also describes the parties' representation at hearings and their use of witnesses.

Chapter 2 reviews the tribunal decisions to determine whether they reveal any patterns or suggest any problems. Particular attention is paid to whether the tribunals were applying the legislation correctly, whether they were adhering to the instructions of higher courts in reaching their decisions, whether there were considerations which seemed to be important to them, and whether the decisions reached by the various tribunals were largely consistent with each other.

Having identified certain problems in the adjudication of claims by the tribunals, Chapter 3 attempts to determine their causes, examining possibilities both within the tribunal panels themselves and in the presentations being made to them by the parties.

The lack of knowledgeable advice and representation appeared to be a widespread and serious problem for complainants. Chapter 4 contains the information developed on this subject.

Chapter 5 analyses success at sex discrimination and equal pay hearings. Statistical analyses are provided to demonstrate the relative importance of those factors which seem very important to success – having a woman on the tribunal panel, having a full-time chairman and presenting witnesses. Findings on the relation of complainants' and respondents' type of representation to their success are also presented.

Chapter 6 summarises the major findings of the study and makes recommendations for changes to minimise or eliminate some of the problems identified. There is also a discussion of the significance which the findings of this study hold for some of the major proposals for change previously made by other commentators.

Notes

1   There are, of course, other significant differences. The American EEOC has jurisdiction over discrimination in employment only; the EOC, over discrimination in all the areas mentioned. The EOC addresses discrimination based on sex only; the American EEOC also concerns itself with discrimination based on race, colour, religion and national origin.

2   Complaints regarding discrimination in all areas other than employment are taken to the County Courts. These, too, must be filed by individuals.

3   EOC *Annual Report* (1976), p.3

4   These Select Committees were set up in 1971 and 1972, to look at proposals for new anti-discrimination legislation introduced, respectively, by Baroness Seear in the House of Lords and by Willie Hamilton MP in the House of Commons. See also Byrne and Lovenduski, (1978) (Vol 1), p131-167. No doubt the American EEOC's 1975 backlog of approximately 120,000 individual charges provided a graphic illustration of the practical difficulties of the potential burden of responsibility for individual complaints. See Schlei and Grossman (1976), p.761.

5   Goodman (1979), p.1-3.

6   Figures from various issues of the *Employment Gazette*.

7   NCCL, (1973).

8   Leonard (1986). From 1976-1983 there were 1,794 applications filed under the SDA 1975. 717 (39%) proceeded to a tribunal hearing, of which 192 (27%) were successful. This was 11% of all SDA 1975 applications. Under the EQPA 1970, from 1976-1983 there were 4,296 applications filed, of which 2,147 (50%) proceeded to a tribunal hearing, where 428 (20%) were successful. This was 10% of all EQPA 1970 applicants. The information is calculated from statistics prepared by the DE.

9   In 1976 there were 1,742 equal pay claims; in 1982, 39. Sex discrimination claims dropped from 243 in 1976 to 150 in 1982.

10   Gregory (1982), identifies lack of informed and sympathetic advice, lack of resources and lack of access to information, and uneven support from trade unions as problems which were discouraging applicants. See also the subsequent study by Graham and Lewis (1985).

11   See, for example, Bindman (1980) (LSG 77:12); Lustgarten (1977); Pannick (1981); and Hepple (1983).

12   Coussins (1976).

13   The notable exception is Coussins (1976). This report assessed the workings of the Acts in their first year, and included information on hearings observed in the first ten months of the legislation.

14   Graham and Lewis (1985).

15   Leonard (1987).

16   The study of complainants under the Race Relations Act 1976 had been undertaken by the CRE; that of unfair dismissal complainants by the (then) Economic and Social Research Council's Industrial Relations Unit at the University of Warwick. See CRE, 1986; this presents the findings of the CRE's study, which involved interviews of 377 individuals who filed

employment discrimination cases with the industrial tribunals in the two-year period July 1978 to June 1980, examining their experiences from filing the claims through to conciliation and/or the tribunal hearing, with particular emphasis on the effect of representation on case outcome: and Dickens, Jones, Weekes and Hart (1985): this study, of 1000 individuals who filed complaints of unfair dismissal between October 1976 and September 1977, used interviews and postal questionnaires with complainants and their related employers to obtain information about the conciliation process, the tribunal hearings, and the results. These two studies cover periods substantially earlier than that covered by this research, which reduces their comparative value. However, they were directly concerned with some of the same issues which prompted this study, and they would be of considerable value to the interested reader.

17   British experts recommended this period on the grounds that after the legislation came into effect in 1975, two or three years elapsed before a good degree of uniformity was introduced into the tribunals' decisions in sex discrimination and equal pay cases, partly as a result of guidance from the EAT on several issues of substantive law and procedure.

18   See Pannick (1985). This provides a comprehensive review of the legislation and the cases decided under it and contains a critical analysis of the shortcomings of the various provisions.

CHAPTER 1

USING THE INDUSTRIAL TRIBUNALS

The Procedure for Making a Claim

Detailed explanation of the history of the industrial tribunals, their various jurisdictions, the process of filing claims with them, and their operations, are available elsewhere.[1] To preface this book, however, a simple explanation is provided of how an individual initiates a claim for equal pay or a claim of sex discrimination in employment, the various stages of the application, certain basic features of tribunal hearings, and what remedies a successful complainant may expect. Several of these topics are discussed at greater length in subsequent chapters; this description will serve simply to provide a basic understanding sufficient to place what follows in context.

Initiating a Claim

Individuals who believe they have been treated less favourably than a person of the other sex with regard to most aspects of employment, initiate a legal challenge to the situation by filing an application with the industrial tribunals, either at a regional office or at the Central Office of Industrial Tribunals in London (or, if in Scotland, in Glasgow). A prescribed application form – the IT-1 – available at employment offices and job centres, elicits the name of the individual bringing the case ("the complainant", or "applicant"), the name of the person or firm she is suing ("the respondent"), and a statement of the claim being made. One or more claims within the tribunals' jurisdictions may be made simultaneously; and it is not uncommon for a complainant to claim her dismissal was both 'unfair' and discriminatory, or to claim both unfair dismissal *and* equal pay for some period prior to the termination of employment.

Joint Applications

Two or more individuals may, with the permission of the tribunal or by agreement with the respondent, bring joint applications to the tribunal. In the early years of the legislation, such multiple-complainant cases were fairly frequent, especially among claims for equal pay.

Time Limits for Filing Claims

There are time limits for filing both sex discrimination and equal pay claims. A claim of sex discrimination in employment must be filed with the tribunals within three months of the act which is complained of. The SDA 1975 does, however, provide that this time limit can be extended by the tribunal if, in all the circumstances of the case, it considers it just and equitable to do so.[2] In practice, this power is rarely used. Britain has the shortest time limit for filing such claims of any country in the European Community.[3]

Greater flexibility exists for equal pay claims, which may be filed at any time during a person's employment and within up to six months after that employment has ceased.[4]

Advice

Many individuals seek advice before or after formally filing a claim. Some obtain advice from the EOC in Manchester; others from their trade union, Citizens' Advice Bureaux and Job Centres.

Representation

Complainants and respondents attend tribunal hearings either by themselves or accompanied by a representative. In the tribunals, representatives need not be legally qualified and in addition to barristers and solicitors, parties use representatives ranging from trade union shop stewards and officials, to individuals from law centres or citizen advisory groups, to friends and relatives. Legal aid is not available for representation at tribunal hearings. However, under the Legal Aid Advice Scheme, an individual who qualifies for Legal Aid may receive up to £50 worth of legal advice, which includes such services as letters written on her behalf, advice on necessary evidence, etc.

The EOC itself is empowered to provide representation for complainants (usually assistance by an outside solicitor or barrister) where

(1)   the case raises a question of principle;
(2)   the case is complex or, for certain other reasons, it is unreasonable to expect the complainant to deal with the case unaided; or
(3)   because of any other special consideration.[5]

However, the Commission grants such assistance to only half of those who request it each year.[6] In addition a good number of complainants each year are represented at their hearings by their trade unions, and a few are represented by individuals from

Citizens' Advice Bureaux or by friends. Nonetheless, over the years nearly half of the complainants under each Act attended hearings without a representative of any sort.[7]

Questions and Replies Procedure

With respect to case preparation, SDA 1975, s.74 is a unique provision. It assists a person who considers they may have been discriminated against 'to decide whether to initiate proceedings and, if he does so, to formulate and present his case in the most effective manner . . .'.[8] A form for this purpose can be sent to the respondent, posing questions about the reasons for his actions, or any other relevant matter, prior to initiating an application or later. The Act also provides that:

> If it appears to the . . . tribunal that the respondent deliberately, and without reasonable excuse, omitted to reply within a reasonable period or that his reply is evasive or equivocal, the . . . tribunal may draw any inference from that fact that it considers just and equitable to draw, including an inference that he commited an unlawful act.[9]

Conciliation and Settlement of Claims

As with claims of unfair dismissal and claims of unfair selection for redundancy, when a claim of sex discrimination or equal pay is filed a copy is sent to ACAS, who may attempt to promote a settlement of the complaint. The ACAS officer will do this either
(1) if requested to do so by both the complainant and the respondent, or
(2) if, even without such requests, the officer considers that there is a reasonable prospect of reaching such a settlement.

Withdrawing an Application

At any time, with or without stating reasons, a complainant may withdraw the complaint about sex discrimination or equal pay. In practice, about one-third of all applicatons are withdrawn, although about a quarter of that number are actually cases in which private settlements were reached by the parties, who do not wish to disclose the fact of the settlement or its terms.[10] The large majority, however, merely represents a decision by the complainant not to proceed further with the claim. The reasons for this significant proportion of withdrawals have been investigated in the study of the concilation process mentioned above.[11]

Types of Tribunal Hearings

Where a complaint is neither settled nor withdrawn, it proceeds to the more formal stages before a tribunal. In many cases, this means simply a single hearing on the full case, at which the parties present their evidence and their witnesses, if any, and the tribunal reaches a decision on the facts in the light of the applicable legislation. In other cases, the parties may have one or more additional contacts with a tribunal, either in person or in writing. The possibilities include:

(1) A pre-hearing assessment, at which the tribunal attempts to clarify the claims and issues presented by a case, often with an eye to determining whether there is actually a case to be answered. Such a hearing may have implications with respect to costs (see *Costs*, below).

(2) A preliminary hearing, held where the respondent or the tribunal staff believe that there may be no jurisdiction to decide the case, e.g., where the application has been filed after the three-month time limit, or where the complainant is not an 'employee' within the definition of the SDA 1975 or the EQPA 1970.

(3) Interlocutory hearings, which include hearings on parties' requests for inspection of documents and hearings to determine triable issues.

(4) A dismissal for want of prosecution, where a case may be dismissed if the complainant does not appear at the scheduled hearing and no explanation is received or obtained by the office of tribunals. A case may also be dismissed for want of prosecution where a complainant has delayed an inordinately long time in accepting a hearing date.

(5) A hearing on compensation or remedy, where a complainant wins the case; the tribunal may itself determine the compensation or other remedy, or it may leave this issue to be agreed by the parties, with a right to return to the tribunal if negotiation fails. A separate hearing on compensation can be held if the parties need time to prepare evidence on that issue, if the parties fail to agree on compensation and return to have the matter decided by the tribunal, or where the complainant invokes tribunal assistance because the employer has simply refused to comply with the tribunal's order.

Procedure at Hearings

There are two points of general importance concerning procedure at a tribunal hearing on a sex discrimination or equal pay claim. The first is that the procedure followed is largely up to the tribunals themselves to determine. Rule 8 of the Industrial Tribunals Rules of Procedure 1980 provides that:

> The tribunal shall conduct the hearing in such a manner as it considers most suitable to the clarification of the issues before it and generally to the just handling of the proceedings; it shall so far as appears to it appropriate seek to avoid formality in its proceedings and it shall not be bound by any enactment or rule of law relating to the admissibility of evidence in proceedings before the courts of law.

The 'informality' of tribunal hearings is widely considered to be one of their major advantages. However the degree of formality varies greatly among tribunals, and opinions differ as to whether informality is in fact of substantial assistance to complainants generally.

The second matter of importance concerning procedure in a sex discrimination or equal pay case is that the complainant has the burden of proof – that is, the complainant must present evidence sufficient to convince the tribunal that discrimination has occurred. The subject of much interest and debate, this rule has been criticised most frequently for being unreasonably burdensome to a complainant in cases such as these, where most of the relevant information will be in the control of the respondent. The details of this debate are presented in Chapter 6; the essential fact at this point being that it is the complainant who must persuade the tribunal by a preponderance of the evidence that the respondent has committed a discriminatory act.

Remedies

In sex discrimination cases, where an industrial tribunal determines that discrimination has occurred, the tribunal may take any of three possible remedial actions which it considers to be 'just and equitable':
(1) an order declaring the rights of the complainant and the respondent in relation to the act to which the complaint relates;
(2) an order requiring the respondent to pay to the complainant compensation of an amount corresponding to any damages he could have been ordered by a county court or by a sheriff court to pay to the complainant if the complaint had fallen to be dealt with there;
(3) a recommendation that the respondent take within a speci-

fied period action appearing to the tribunal to be practicable for the purpose of obviating or reducing the adverse effect on the complainant of any act of discrimination to which the complaint relates.[12]

The amount of compensation may not exceed that permitted for unfair dismissal.

In addition to compensation for 'employment loss', e.g., the loss of the complainant's job or loss of a job opportunity, damages with respect to an act of unlawful discrimination may include compensation for injury to feelings whether or not they include compensation under any other head.[13]

In claims for equal pay, where a tribunal determines that a complainant does deserve pay equal to a 'comparator,' it may award equal pay; where appropriate it may award arrears of remuneration or damages in respect of the work for up to two years prior to the date on which the complainant instituted proceedings.

Costs

Generally speaking, parties to the tribunals bear their own costs. However, where the tribunal finds that a party 'has in bringing or conducting the proceedings acted frivolously, vexatiously or otherwise unreasonably, the tribunal may make an order'. (Rule 11(1)). Tribunals have, for example, awarded costs against respondents because they behaved unreasonably in not admitting liability earlier. More often, however, this provision is of concern to complainants. At a pre-hearing assessment, used where the tribunal doubts that there is actually a case to be answered, it may warn the complainant that if at the full hearing the claim is found to be frivolous or vexatious, they may be ordered to pay costs.

Enforcement

The industrial tribunals themselves do not have coercive powers, that is, powers actually to compel a respondent to pay the compensation the tribunal has awarded or to take the action the tribunal has recommended. Where a respondent fails to comply with a recommendation, the tribunal's only power is to increase the amount of compensation to be paid or, if no compensation has been ordered, to order it.[14]

Where a respondent still does not comply and further action is needed, complainants face different situations depending upon whether they are in England and Wales or in Scotland. In Scotland, tribunal orders are virtually 'instantly enforceable': if not complied with, they can be certified by the Secretary of the

Industrial Tribunals after which they can be executed directly by a sheriff officer. In England and Wales, the procedure is more complicated and more costly.[15] A complainant must 'register' the tribunal decision in a county court, usually paying a separate fee. The complainant ultimately receives from the county court an enforceable order based upon the tribunal decision, which can be used to initiate coercive action against the employer.

Review and Appeal

In specified limited circumstances,[16] either party may within 14 days after a tribunal decision apply for a review of the decision by the same tribunal. Such applications are often decided by the chairman alone; though where review is actually granted, or a further hearing held, it occurs before the full panel.

Within six weeks of the date on which a tribunal decision is sent to the parties, either party may register an appeal with the EAT. However, appeals may be taken only upon questions of law, such as the correct interpretation of a statutory provision. Questions of fact, such as the question of the credibility of witnesses, rest firmly with the tribunals, and are not subject to appeal.

A Profile of the Hearings

This section provides a brief overall picture of tribunal activity on sex discrimination and equal pay claims from 1980-1982; a description of the complainants and respondents; and information about the parties' representation at hearings and their use of witnesses.

Overall Tribunal Activity

In the three-year period from January 1980-December 1982, some 770 men and women filed complaints of sex discrimination in employment or for equal pay. Typical of complainants since 1976, approximately one-third ultimately withdrew their applications and another third reached settlements with the employer concerned. Only about one-third therefore actually pursued their claims through to a full tribunal hearing. A review of the files maintained by COIT and the EOC produced the following profile of tribunal activity on cases in the period:[17]

Table 1.1 *Profile of Tribunal Activity 1980-1982*

Preliminary hearings	26
Interlocutory hearings and requests for inspection of documents[18]	6
Dismissals for want of prosecution	12

Table 1.1 (*cont*)

Decisions on case merits	227
Hearings on compensation/remedy	12
Applications for review[18]	15
Total decisions	**298**

Multiple Claims

Over one-third of the 227 cases decided on the merits of the claim involved more than a single sex discrimination or equal pay claim. Most common among the 78 multiple-claim cases were those which combined a sex discrimination or equal pay claim with a claim of unfair dismissal (57 cases); in four other cases, complainants claimed sex discrimination *and* equal pay *and* unfair dismissal; and in a further four cases, the sex discrimination or equal pay claim was joined with a claim of racial discrimination. With so many cases involving more than one claim, the total of 227 cases with full hearings actually represents 249 separate *claims* of sex discrimination or equal pay.

Complainants and Respondents

The 227 hearing decisions from England and Wales and Scotland were reviewed to determine complainants' sex, type of claim, occupation, and the incidence of multiple-complainant cases. The Scottish hearings were so few in number during this period that they were generally not amenable to detailed statistical breakdown; such breakdowns are therefore provided only for the 215 decisions from England and Wales.

Complainants' Sex

With slight yearly variations, complainants at 80% of the hearings in England and Wales were women; similarly in Scotland, in 75% of the cases heard, the complainants were women.

Type of Discrimination Alleged

Women and men complained about different types of discrimination. The great majority of hearings on men's claims (23 out of 39) concerned discrimination in recruitment and hiring; men brought very few equal pay claims. For women, hearings on discrimimation in dismissal were the largest single category; hearings on discrimination in promotion, transfer, and recruitment were also numerous. Table 1.2 provides the figures for hearings in England and Wales; the numbers of Scottish hearings are noted separately in parentheses.

Table 1.2 *Type of discrimination alleged at SDA and EQPA hearings 1980-1982 by complainants' sex*

	Total	Men	Women
Sex Discrimination Claims:			
Recruitment, Hiring	40 (4)	23	17
Promotion, Transfer	30 (2)	2	28
Dismissal	53 (3)	8	45
Victimisation	10 (1)	0	10
Other	29 (1)	6	23
Equal Pay Claims:			
Grading scheme	17	0	17
Other	55 (4)	8	47
Total All Claims:	234 (15)	47	187

Number of Complainants per Case

In the early years of the equality legislation, multiple-complainant cases were fairly frequent, especially in claims for equal pay. However, in 1980-1982 these occurred infrequently. Of the 215 cases heard in England and Wales, 194 (90%) were brought by a single complainant, 13 (6%) involved two complainants, and eight (4%) involved three complainants or more. Of the 21 multiple-complainant cases, 11 involved sex discrimination claims, eight involved equal pay claims, and two included both types of claims.

Complainants' Occupation

The employment status of complainants at the hearings can be categorised into five major groups:[19]
(1)   Professional and managerial occupations[20]
(2)   Clerical and related occupations[21]
(3)   Selling occupations[22]
(4)   Personal services; all manual occupations[23]
(5)   Other occupations[24]

The occupations of complainants with hearings on sex discrimination claims were different from those with hearings on equal pay claims. Table 1.3 provides the figures for the 219 claims for which the occupation of the complainant was stated in the hearing decision.

Table 1.3 *Occupations of complainants at SDA and EQPA hearings, 1980-1982*

	Sex discrimination claims		Equal pay claims	
	No	%	No	%
Professional/managerial	48	32	16	23
Clerical, related	27	18	19	28
Sales	17	11	8	12
All manual	59	39	25	37
Total	151	100	68	100

Respondents' Type of Business and Workforce Size

Although the respondents' type of business can usually be determined from the tribunal decision, information on workforce size is elusive. Tribunal decisions normally do not contain this information and statistics maintained by the DE are unhelpful.[25] Where possible, therefore, information in Dun and Bradstreet publications[26] was used to estimate workforce size; the analysis must, however, be regarded as somewhat imprecise.

Table 1.4 shows the type of business and the workforce size of the respondents at the 215 hearings held in England and Wales in the three-year period examined.

Table 1.4 *Type of business and workforce size of respondents at SDA and EQPA hearings, 1980-1982*

	No	%
Central government departments	10	5
National Health Service Hospitals and Area Health Authorities	8	4
Borough, City, and County Councils	20	9
Nationalised State Industries	12	5
Registered Companies (by number of employees)		
More than 1,000	36	17
500-999	12	5
100-499	20	9
50-99	12	5
20-49	11	5
Less than 20	3	1
Not known	73	34
Total	217*	

* In two cases, the Manpower Services Commission was a co-respondent.

Of the 217 respondents reviewed, 50 (24%) were central or local government entities or government owned or partly-owned industries; 48 (22%) were registered companies with 500 employees or more; 20 (9%) were companies with 100-499 employees; and only 3 (1%) were companies with fewer than 20 employees. Using informal indicators for the companies whose size could not be determined precisely, it appeared that another 38 (18%) respondents had workforces of substantial size.

The clear picture is that the overwhelming number of complainants who had hearings on sex discrimination and equal pay applications during this period were against either government entities or government-owned or partly-owned industries, or against large registered companies. Of the 38 applications which concerned central government, local government, health authorities, and hospitals, 30 were sex discrimination claims while only eight were claims for equal pay. The distribution of sex discrimination and equal pay cases among private respondents was not analysed, since the workforce size of a substantial number of these could only be estimated or was unknown.

Witnesses and Representation at Tribunal Hearings
Use of Witnesses at Hearings

The hearing decisions were used to determine how often complainants and respondents presented witnesses at their tribunal hearings.

Table 1.5 *Complainants' and respondents' use of witnesses at SDA and EQPA hearings, 1980-1982*

	Decisions stating the number of witnesses	The party only testified	One witness	Two witness	Three or more witnesses
Complainants	205	149 (73%)	32 (16%)	11 (5%)	13 (6%)
Respondents	189	82 (43%)	50 (26%)	34 (18%)	23 (12%)

Clearly, respondents took witnesses to hearings much more frequently than complainants. Complainants presented testimony in addition to their own in only 27% of cases whereas respondents presented witnesses in addition to their 'primary witness' 56% of the time. Respondents also took witnesses in greater numbers: they presented additional testimony from one person almost twice as often as complainants; additional testimony from two people over three times as often; and additional testimony from three or more people twice as often.

Sex Discrimination and Equal Pay Cases Compared The number of witnesses complainants presented varied little between sex discrimination and equal pay claims. Respondents, however, showed distinctly different patterns in their use of witnesses, taking more witnesses more often to hearings on sex discrimination claims. Respondents took one or more witnesses to just over 60% of the hearings on sex discrimination claims, but to only 44% of the hearings on equal pay claims.

Witnesses' Sex It was possible, with most of the decisions, to determine the sex of the parties' witnesses. At only one hearing in four did respondents' witnesses include a woman, leaving the (mostly women) complainants opposed by a set of all male witnesses in three out of every four hearings. In addition, 70% of complainants' own witnesses were males.

Representation

Among questions most frequently asked about equal rights cases in the tribunal are those about representation: what types of representatives are used and how often? Does the type of representation affect the outcome? Providing accurate answers to these questions is very difficult, since records maintained on representation are unhelpful in several respects. The ACAS/DE statistics, recorded in the first instance by ACAS personnel and compiled and published by the DE, are of questionable accuracy and for years have been widely regarded as unreliable.[27] In addition, since they record information in terms of complainants rather than cases, these statistics offer quite skewed pictures for those years in which there were multiple-complainant cases.[28] COIT maintains information on representation at tribunals which is regarded as highly accurate; but it does not distinguish sex discrimination and equal pay cases from those of other jurisdictions.

The tribunal hearing decisions were of very limited assistance in themselves. Unlike those from Scotland, where information on the parties' representation is recorded on the first page of every tribunal decision, decisions in England and Wales do not routinely include such information; in fact, of the decisions reviewed in this study, one-third did not state whether the complainant was represented, and almost half did not state whether the respondents were represented.

In an attempt to remedy this situation this study developed other information to supplement the DE statistics.

COIT statistics on overall representation in the tribunals are provided for comparative purposes.

Complainants' Representation 1976-1983

By 1980-1982, there was a dramatic decrease in the number of sex discrimination and equal pay applications to the tribunals and a corresponding decrease in the number of hearings on those claims. Therefore the most accurate view of complainants' representation at such hearings is provided by the statistics for the entire eight-year period for which they were available, i.e., 1976-1983. These show:

Table 1.6 *Complainants' type of representation at SDA and EQPA hearings, 1976-1983*

	SDA (717)	EQPA (2,147)
Solicitor, Counsel*	27%	8%
Trade Union*	25%	42%
Self	32%	14%
Other	11%	4%
Rep. not present	2%	0
Type rep. unknown	3%	32%

Source: DE Statistics, Tables 2(G)
*There is apparently no clear rule for classifying solicitors who are employed by trades unions; they may have been included in either of the categories indicated. This is true wherever DE statistics are quoted in this study. The annual data is provided in Appendix 1.

It is important to note that these are figures concerning *individual complainants*. However in equal pay cases, especially in the first few years of the legislation, cases often involved multiple complainants: even as many as 50 would be involved in a single hearing. Therefore, the percentage of *hearings* where complainants had trade union representation would be much lower than the percentage of the absolute numbers of individuals involved. Unfortunately, it is impossible from existing records to determine the correct figures accurately.[29]

By 1980-1982 legal representation at sex discrimination hearings had increased to one-third of all complainants. Trade union representation accounted for only 17%, and self-represented complainants constituted 36% of the whole. At equal pay hearings, legal representation had risen dramatically to 30% of complainants, trade union representatives handled only 14% of hearings, and self-represented complainants were 39% of the whole. The complete figures are provided in Appendix 2.

All Tribunal Jurisdictions COIT statistics on complainants' type of representation at hearings in all the tribunals' jurisdictions during 1980-1982 showed 40% were self-represented, 34% had legal representation, 17% had trade union representation, and 8% had other types of representatives.[30]

Support from the EOC The SDA 1975 empowers the EOC to assist individuals who are actual or prospective complainants
(1) where the case raises a question of principle; or
(2) where it is unreasonable to expect the applicant to deal with the case unaided because of its complexity or because of the complainant's position in relation to the respondent or another person involved in the matter; or
(3) because of any other special consideration.[31]

Such assistance may include providing advice; attempting to procure a settlement of any matter in dispute; arranging for the advice or assistance of a solicitor or counsel; and arranging for representation by any person, including a solicitor or counsel. In England and Wales, the EOC supported legal assistance at industrial tribunal hearings for 12 complainants in 1980, 14 in 1981, and 15 in 1982. In Scotland, it supported representation at tribunal hearings for two complainants in 1980, one in 1981 and three in 1982.[32] In addition, the EOC supported representation at about six preliminary hearings in 1980-1982.

Respondents' Representation 1976-1983

The DE does not record information on respondents' representation at hearings on equal pay claims, nor was information available on their representation at sex discrimination hearings in 1980. Table 1.7 summarises the DE statistic on respondents' representation at 620 hearings on sex discrimination claims from 1976-1983, excluding 1980.

Table 1.7   *Respondents' type of representation at SDA and EQPA hearings, 1976-1983 (excl. 1980)*

Solicitor/Counsel	48%
Personnel/Industrial Relations Mgt.	28%
Other Management	13%
Employers' Association	3%
Other	3%
Representative not present	2%
Not known	3%
Total	620

Source: DE Statistics, Table 6

All Tribunal Jurisdictions   According to COIT the type of representation respondents had in cases from all jurisdictions in the period 1980-1982 was 49% legal representatives; 8% employers' organisations; 5% other types; and 38% 'none.' 'None' is used to indicate that the employer is represented by a non-legally qualified employee, such as a personnel manager; presumably, then, this category corresponds to the two DE categories which refer to managerial personnel.[33]

The Balance of Representation

The review of the 215 tribunal decisions yielded 70 decisions in which the type of representation for *both* the complainant and the respondent could be determined. These included two interesting groupings: one involving 58 cases, where the respondent was represented by a solicitor or by counsel, and another involving 33 cases, where the complainant was not represented or had a lay representative (husband, father, CAB). Table 1.8 provides the profile of the representation of these groups.

Table 1.8   *Patterns in parties' relative types of representation at SDA and EQPA hearings, 1980-1982*

No of cases	Complainant representative	Respondent representative
24	Legal	Legal
13	Trade Union	Legal
13	Self	Legal
4	Husband, father, friend	Legal
4	CAB, Law Centre, etc	Legal
10	Self	Manager
2	Self	Employer's Association, Adviser

These figures and those on parties' representation generally, suggest that many complainants, and their representatives if they have them, are faced with respondents whose representatives are professionals, and many of whom are skilled at representation.

Notes

1   See, for example, Goodman (1979).
2   SDA 1975, s.76(5).
3   Corcoran and Donnelly (1984).
4   EQPA 1970, s.2(4).
5   SDA 1975, s.75.
6   This information is contained in each *Annual Report* of the EOC.
7   Leonard (1986).
8   SDA 1975, s.74(1).
9   SDA 1975, s.74(2)(b).
10   Leonard (1986).
11   Graham and Lewis (1985).
12   SDA 1975, s.65.
13   SDA 1975, s.66(4).
14   SDA 1975, s.65(3).
15   An investigation into this aspect of complainants' experiences was included in a study of successful sex discrimination and equal pay complainants from 1980 to 1984, undertaken by this author with funding from the EOC. The report on the project was submitted to the EOC. See Leonard (1987).
16   (1) A tribunal shall have power to review and to revoke or vary by certificate under the chairman's hand any decision on the grounds that—
(a) the decision was wrongly made as a result of an error on the part of the tribunal staff; or
(b) a party did not receive notice of the proceedings leading to the decision; or
(c) the decision was made in the absence of a party or person entitled to be heard; or
(d) new evidence has become available since the making of the decision provided that its existence could not have been reasonably known of or foreseen; or
(e) the interests of justice require such a review.
      (2) An application for the purposes of paragraph (1) of this Rule may be made at the hearing. If the application is not made at the hearing, such application shall be made to the Secretary of the Tribunals at any time from the date of the hearing until 14 days after the date on which the decision was sent to the parties and must be in writing stating the grounds in full. (Rule 10: *Industrial Tribunal Rules of Procedure 1980*).
17   The table includes only those decisions which actually addressed a sex discrimination or equal pay claim. It does *not* include two types of cases which have some importance: cases which were filed with a sex discri-

mination or equal pay claim which was withdrawn or not pursued at the hearing, and a few cases in which there was an obvious sex discrimination or equal pay claim that was not raised by the applicant. Some decisions are announced orally by the tribunal chairman at the end of the hearing; in others, the tribunal 'reserves' its decision, and the written decision announces the outcome to the parties. For the sake of uniformity, the 'decision date' used here is the date the decision was certified and sent to the parties – a date which is indicated on each decision.

18   The figures on these decisions are likely to be less accurate than on others because the ROITS do not regularly send them to the EOC, and even in the COIT files they are often not clearly marked as sex discrimination or equal pay cases.

19   See *Classification of Occupations* and *Directory of Occupational Titles* (HMSO, 1972).

20   'Professional and Managerial' includes jobs in DE classification I-VI as follows:

I   Managerial occupations (General management);
II   Professional and related occupations supporting management and administration;
III   Professional and related occupations in education, welfare and health;
IV   Literary, artistic and sports occupations;
V   Professional and related occupations in science, engineering, technology and similiar fields;
VI   Managerial occupations (excluding general management).

21   'Clerical and related' includes jobs in DE Classifications VII, Clerical and related occupations.

22   'Sales' includes jobs in DE Classification VII, Selling Occupations

23   'All Manual' includes jobs in DE Classifications IX – XVII, as follows:

IX   Security and protective service occupations;
X   Catering, cleaning, hairdressing, and other personal service occupations;
XI   Farming, fishing and related occupations;
XII   Materials processing occupations (excluding metal);
XIII Making and repairing occupations (excluding metal and electrical);
XIV   Processing, making and repairing and related occupations (metal and electrical);
XV   Painting, repetitive assembling, product inspecting, packaging and related occupations;
XVI   Construction, mining and related occupations;
XVII Transport operating, materials moving and storing, and related occupations.

24   'Other Occupations' includes jobs in DE Classification XVII, 'Miscellaneous occupations and occupations for which no appropriate classification existed'. It also includes those few cases in which the tribunal decision does not state what the complainant's job was. This category was not included in the table.

25   A recent government survey found that a significant number of firms categorised as 'small' by ACAS were actually small establishments which formed part of a large company.

26   Dun and Bradstreet (1983); Dun and Bradstreet International (1983).

27   Hawkes and Smith (1981).

28   One example will illustrate the problem: DE statistics for SDA 1975 cases in 1976 show a total of 174 complainants; yet it appears probable that one case involved 68 complainants handled by a trade union representative. Counted by complainants, the statistics show 90 out of 174 with trade union representation, just over 50%. But if they are (more appropriately) considered as a single case, then the trade union representation falls to 21%. Since multi-complainant cases were larger and more frequent in the EQPA 1970 cases than in the SDA 1975 cases, the distortions are even greater for that jurisdiction. Multi-complainant cases were frequent in the early years of the legislation, and therefore they make figures on the trends in representation somewhat unreliable. Accordingly that information is provided in Appendix 1. However, during 1980 to 1982 the number of such cases was minimal. A partial adjustment is reflected in the EQPA figures in Appendix 2.

29   For more detailed analysis of complainants' representation under both Acts, see Leonard (1986).

30   Information provided by COIT in London. The figures are drawn from an analysis of all cases heard over a four-week period in October/November each year.

31   SDA 1975, s.75.

32   The EOC *Annual Reports* (1980-1982), however, show 'legal assistance granted' concerning fully 222 tribunal applications, and advice granted for 39 tribunal applications.

33   Information provided by COIT. The figures are drawn from an analysis of all cases heard over a four-week period in October/November each year.

CHAPTER 2

THE ADJUDICATION OF CLAIMS

To develop an understanding of how the tribunals are deciding claims of sex discrimination and equal pay, this study relied primarily upon case decisions. Observations at hearings served to suggest lines of inquiry and to confirm or modify conclusions reached on the basis of the far larger sample provided by the written decisions. In all, 265 decisions were reviewed during the period 1980-1982, including decisions from preliminary hearings, hearings on case merits, and hearings on compensation. The analysis revealed one difficulty worth mentioning: the variable standard and content of the decisions. Some decisions were very informative: they stated clearly who the parties were, whether they were represented and, if so, by whom; described who testified at the hearing on behalf of each party and, usually briefly, what they said; summarised the important evidence and its source; weighed the evidence before the tribunal; and stated the tribunal's findings, their conclusions and their reasons for them. Yet many decisions omitted or declined to do one or more of these things; some were so cryptic that it was not clear what was claimed to have been discriminatory and why the tribunal dismissed the claim. This is demonstrated by the following findings:

Most decisions stated clearly who the parties were and what they claimed. Others did not: several either failed to identify the complainant's job or to provide even minimal details of the respondent's type of business or, more frequently, to state the nature of the claim.

Sixty-four of the 215 decisions stated whether the parties were represented (and, if so, by whom) in addition to who testified at the hearings. One hundred and fifty-one (70%) did not contain this information. It was thus *very* common to read a decision without knowing whether the parties were represented, and without knowing who had provided the evidence to which it referred.

A substantial number of tribunals did not relate the evidence presented at the hearing; 62 decisions made specific reference to testimony, documents, 'section 74' responses, or other exhibits, but did not describe their substance. While some tribunals took pains to summarise evidence in detail – even where it had been voluminous – others specifically declined to do so.

Even where decisions did summarise the evidence, they often did not specify who had presented it or whether it was testimonial or documentary. Only 77 decisions stated the *sources* of information considered; the other 138 did not. Certain decisions were so devoid of 'clues' about the source of information that it was impossible to tell whether a complainant or respondent had conceded a point or had contested it.

Many decisions include judgements on the credibility of witnesses, although, of the 134 which mentioned issues of credibility, only 65 stated the tribunals' reasons for the various judgements made.

In six cases, the facts were agreed by the parties, or the decision primarily involved a question of law. Of the 206 cases in which there was conflicting evidence to be weighed, only 111 described this analysis in the decision.

Twenty decisions – almost 10% – did not state the reasons for the decision reached on the claim.

The significance of these differences for this study was two-fold: first, certain types of information – such as representation of the parties – was not sufficiently reliable that it could be used. Secondly, in analysing the tribunals' decision-making, the question of what tribunals had or had not done or considered had to be approached with great caution. It was felt that the study must rely primarily upon what tribunals said they *had* done or *had* considered; it could not reliably infer that a tribunal had failed to do or consider something simply because it was not mentioned in the decision.

Adopting this approach, five subjects were chosen for detailed analysis:
(1) whether the tribunals had correctly understood and applied the statutory provisions of the SDA 1975 and the EQPA 1970;
(2) whether they had applied the legal standard called for by those Acts;
(3) whether they had demanded 'clear and specific' explanations from employers who had allegedly discriminated, as required in these cases by the EAT;
(4) whether, in reaching their decisions, there were particular considerations which they found important or persuasive;
(5) whether the decisions reached by the various tribunals were generally consistent.

The findings on these topics are presented below.

Legal Errors

While a number of the tribunal decisions demonstrated a knowledge of sex discrimination and equal pay legislation, some tribunals clearly misunderstood and/or misapplied the SDA 1975 and the EQPA 1970, or were unaware of their provisions.

Applying the Wrong Law

For example, one tribunal dismissed a claim of sex discrimination in recruitment because:

> . . . [the employer stated] that the only people he employs for more than 16 hours a week at the public house are two people in the bar. There is no reason whatsoever to disbelieve this. Therefore, his estalishment is within the provisions of section 6, subsection (3) of the Sex Discrimination Act 1975, and therefore, the allegations of sexual discrimination cannot apply to employment in his establishment. *(Mr J P Murphy v Wolsey Tavern)*

This is incorrect. The application of the SDA 1975 is *not* limited to weekly employment over certain hours, though such a limitation does exist in the Employment Protection (Consolidation) Act 1978. The exclusion of s.6(3) did not necessarily apply.

Direct and Indirect Discrimination

In addition to prohibiting less favourable treatment of women or men because of their sex, the SDA 1975 prohibits 'indirect' discrimination, that is, different treatment which occurs because a requirement or condition which appears neutral on its face, has a disproportionate negative effect upon one sex or the other.[1] Accordingly, in deciding an allegation of indirect discrimination, the tribunal must determine in the first instance whether a 'condition', for example a criterion used in selection for redundancy – is more difficult for individuals of one sex to comply with than for those of the other. Even where this is the case, the discriminatory requirement will be permitted as 'lawful' discrimination where the employer can show the requirement is 'justifiable.'

The definition of what will be considered 'justifiable' has undergone considerable change in recent years, but for most of the period covered in this study it had been fairly strictly described by the EAT as follows:

It may be helpful if we add a word of detail about what we consider to be the right approach to this question. First, the onus of proof was upon the party asserting this proposition, in this case the [respondent] Post Office. Secondly, it is a heavy onus in the sense that at the end of the day the Industrial Tribunal must be satisfied that the case is a genuine one where it can be said that the requirement or condition is necessary. Thirdly, in deciding whether the employer has discharged the onus, the Industrial Tribunal should take into account all the circumstances including the discriminatory effect of the requirement or condition if it is permitted to continue. Fourthly, it is necessary to weigh the need for the requirement or condition against that effect. Fifthly, it is right to distinguish between a requirement or condition which is necessary and one which is merely convenient and for this purpose it is relevant to consider whether the employer can find some other and non-discriminatory method of achieving his object.[2]

Yet one tribunal, addressing a claim that selecting employees for redundancy partly on the basis of whether they were classified as 'skilled' under the national agreement in industry, apparently understood neither the concept of 'disproportionate impact' nor that of 'justifiability'. It rejected the claim of indirect discrimination, stating:

If it be argued that the breach lies within Section 1(b) of the Act, again in our view the allegation must fail because whilst the women could not have been "skilled time served" so as to be retained and [were] thereby unable to comply with such a requirement (Section 1(b) (i)) we hold on the facts that within Section 1(b) (ii) the respondents have shown the said requirement to be justifiable irrespective of the sex of the applicants in so far as it was commercially sound to retain the most skilled, namely "time served skilled," and the requirement applied and trapped in the web of redundancy many men who were skilled non-time served as were the applicants. *(Delia O'Brien v Schreiber Furniture Ltd)*

The tribunal looked neither at the question of disproportionate impact upon women nor at the 'need' for the use of this classification, which it even noted was not one applied with complete even-handedness.

In another case, having concluded that the respondents' arrangements for recruitment had discriminated against the complainant, the tribunal quoted the section of the SDA 1975 which provides for damages:

> Section 66(3) says that as respects unlawful discrimination no award of damages shall be made if the respondent proves that the requirement or condition was not applied with the intention of treating the claimant unfavourably on the grounds of his sex or marital status as the case may be. *(Mrs Clark v Elcoats Insurance (Ipswich) Ltd)*

The tribunal found the respondent had not intended to discriminate and declined to award damages to the complainant. Plainly, however, the tribunal was unaware that the provision cited relates only to instances of *indirect* discrimination and not to *direct* discrimination as was proved in that case.

Employers' Intentions

In deciding an application claiming sex discrimination in hiring, one tribunal wrote:

> The respondents did not deny that the alleged act of discrimination had occurred by a member of staff in their part-time employment. Nevertheless, as soon as the act was drawn to his attention Mr Blackwell did his utmost to remedy the situation. He attempted to telephone the applicant on three occasions, was in verbal communication with an ACAS representative, and communicated his willingness to interview the applicant to the Central Office of the Industrial Tribunals who would have sent the papers to the applicant . . . The tribunal accepted Mr Blackwell's evidence that, if she had contacted him, the present situation would not have arisen. Accordingly, the tribunal unanimously found, as a question of fact, that no sex discrimination was intended in accordance with Section 6(1)(a) of the Sex Discrimination Act 1975. *(Mrs Newman v Alistair Black Ltd)*

On this basis, the tribunal dismissed the application. The disposition is obviously incorrect, since intent is irrelevant to the question whether discrimination occurred. On these facts, it appears it might have been appropriate for the tribunal to find discrimination had occurred, but to award no damages; importing a question of 'intent' clearly is not correct.

Genuine Occupational Qualifications

There were examples of considerable confusion about the concept of a genuine occupational qualification provided in the SDA 1975[3] which allows an employer to hire only men (or only women) for a particular post. One involved a case where a male care assistant applied for a position with a nursing home. He claimed the matron had refused to interview him, stating she wanted a woman for the job. The complainant had found employment as a care assistant elsewhere by the time the tribunal hearing was held and consequently did not attend the hearing. He did, however, send a representative and two written statements. The respondent's matron testified that she had no recollection of speaking to the complainant. The tribunal accepted her testimony and then went further to determine whether in any event, the matron was entitled to consider only women for the post. In so doing, the tribunal must have been thinking of the section of the Act which provides that being a woman is a genuine occupational qualification where the establishment concerned is one for persons requiring special care, supervision, or attention, where those persons are all women and it is reasonable that the job should not be held by a man; or where the holder of the job provides certain personal services which can most effectively be provided by a woman. In this case, the tribunal decided that being a woman *was* a genuine occupational qualification for the job of care assistant. This holding was in spite of the fact that the matron had also testified that the home *did* care for men, having in recent years had four men out of a total of 14 residents; and in spite of the matron's testimony that a different male applicant *had* been asked to interview for this particular post! *(Mr Stubbs v B and R J Hughesdon)*.

Sex-Based General Assumptions

It is a basic tenet of the anti-discrimination legislation that it is discriminatory to take actions (recruitment, promotion, dismissal, etc.) based on sex-based general assumptions about a person's abilities rather than upon relevant individualised assessment or, in certain cases, upon relevant previous experience. A few tribunals rightly recognised this and found sex discrimination had occurred where employers had dismissed or failed to interview individuals because of assumptions based upon their sex, e.g. the assumption that a young mother should be home with her children and that, as a woman, she would not move to take up her employment. *(Mrs Shirley Ali Khan v Kent Country Nurseries Ltd)*; or the assumption that a woman did not have the physical strength necessary for handling containers in a warehouse.*(Miss Kerr v Clyde Factors (Electrical) Ltd)*. However, there were several tribunals which appeared to be quite unaware of the discriminatory possibilities of sex-based assumptions. In fact, there were a number of tribunals which not only accepted but expressed agreement with generalised assumptions about women which were offered to explain an employer's actions, among them, the following:

> We find that the respondents were developing their business by appointing, as a matter of policy, persons to be managers who had the qualifications they looked for in a manager. The applicant did not have those qualifications. For one thing she was unable to do what was required of managers, namely to go out in the evenings, and collect rentals from meters in the homes of hirers, this, as we accept, being a job quite unsuitable for a woman. *(Miss Vickers v N W Electronics (Bradford) Ltd)*

> In addition to the work which was carried out in manufacturing the articles for sale by the means of moulds there was also the work of making the moulds and patterns themselves and ensuring that at all material times they were kept in good condition. The moulds would be kept in good condition by having them buffed from time to time by use of a mechanical buffing machine. The buffer would tend to kick from time to time and consequently the machine had to be held firmly whilst in operation. The respondents considered that this was work primarily suited for a man as opposed to women and we would not quarrel with that viewpoint. *(Mrs Greenhalgh v Grantura Plastics Ltd)*

> The respondent agreed at that time to promote either lady, if satisfied that it would be safe to allow her to do the work required in the men's establishment. Accordingly, each lady was required, as a condition of such promotion, to establish by medical evidence that she was physically capable of doing this work and thereafter successfully to acquire the requisite experience in it by carrying it out for one year (the normal qualifying period for men being four years for new postulants for Grade 10). That offer of access to opportunities for promotion remains available. The respondent was justified in making way for conditions to promotion. It has satisfied us that they are:
> (1) reasonable conditions;
> (2) determined by safety considerations and by prudent and proper concern for the physical well-being and

safety of the ladies themselves and not imposed by way of discrimination against them on the ground of sex. *(Miss Fuller and Mrs Hannis v Paxman Diesels Ltd)*

If, as appears from the decisions, these were assumptions made without reference to facts about the particular complainant involved, they certainly run afoul of the legislation.

Other tribunals made comments which, if not actually antagonistic to the equality legislation, seem unsympathetic to its spirit, including:

> We were impressed by the attitude of the applicant towards her job. When she left to have a baby she chose not to give the notice which would entitle her to the right to return now enjoyed by pregnant employees. *(Mrs Hayward v Keg Services Ltd)*

And:

> It is right to say that the applicant created an extremely favourable impression upon all of us. She was in no way militant. On the contrary, she was plainly extremely emotionally upset as a result of what had occurred. *(Miss King v Amey Roadstone Corp Ltd)*

Other Errors about Statutory Provisions

Other examples include tribunals which did not understand that 'discrimination in access to opportunities for promotion'[4] is a separate claim from 'discrimination in selection for promotion';[5] did not understand the concept of a grading scheme that was sex discriminatory *in operation*;[6] and misunderstood the law concerning claims of equal pay with a successor.[7]

Applying an Incorrect Legal Standard

A more pervasive and possibly more disturbing error is the failure of the tribunals to apply the correct legal standard in sex discrimination and equal pay cases.

Both the SDA 1975 and the EQPA 1970 confer 'comparative' rights, i.e., that an individual of one sex must be treated equally with individuals of the other sex similarly situated.[8] In most cases therefore, the question for the tribunal is whether the complainant was treated *less favourably* than a member of the opposite sex similarly situated and whether the reason for the less favourable treatment was their sex. This is fundamentally different from the tribunals' inquiry in claims of unfair dismissal or unfair selection for redundancy, in which the tribunal asks whether the dismissal or the selection of the complainant was 'reasonable' or 'fair' given all the circumstances. Unfortunately the tribunals in a very substantial number of decisions appeared to also apply this 'reasonableness' or 'fairness' standard to sex discrimination and equal pay cases. For example, in one case a female complainant claimed the financial arrangements for her job were less favourable than those for men with similar positions in the company. One particular claim was that she should have been given a company car rather than just remuneration for her mileage. The tribunal wrote:

> . . . the applicant considered that she ought to have a company car. In the past she has been getting her driving expenses for what appear to have been very substantial miles run week by week. She says that she had asked for this on several occasions in the past, but that she had been given to understand by the company chairman that he did not agree that women should have a company car at all. It seems to us to be of little importance whether her car was a company car provided for her or whether, alternatively, she ran her own car and was given a mileage allowance. Running the miles she was doing week by week, her mileage allowance must have come to a very substantial sum and we cannot think that she really has any complaint on that score. *(Mrs Dungworth v Colnoll Engineering Ltd)*

The tribunal did *not* ask the proper question under the SDA, i.e., whether male employees in the complainant's position were treated differently. It simply dismissed the claim on the basis of its own opinion that mileage allowance 'was just as good' as use of a company car, an error particularly unfortunate in view of the allegation that the company chairman felt that women should not have company cars at all.

In another case, a young man had been dismissed on his second day as a cashier because of a shortage of £3 at the till. At the tribunal he testified that his supervisor had said she wanted a woman for the job and had in fact replaced him with a woman; he claimed his dismissal was discriminatory on the basis of sex. The tribunal did not address and answer the appropriate question (whether *women* 'trainees' would be dismissed immediately for a till shortage of £3 in the first days of their job). It simply held the dismissal was 'reasonable' and justified, and dismissed the application *(Mr Lydon v CD British Telecommunications and Reliance Service Bureau Ltd)*.

In a third case, a female showroom manager claimed sex discrimination in hiring by the British Gas Corporation. She and two other women were interviewed for the position of manager at another showroom but the job was given to a male applicant. The complainant claimed sex discrimination in the way the respondents afforded women access to opportunities for promotion. The complainant introduced statistics to support her contention that there was sex discrimination within her region. She provided evidence that although female showroom managers outnumbered male showroom managers when considering *all categories* of management, nonetheless, in the *most senior grades*, men outnumbered women nationally and in her region men outnumbered women four to one. This, she argued was evidence of discrimination against women in promotion. This was the tribunal's analysis of the information:

> . . . In the Essex area, 11 (showroom managers) were male and nine were female. These figures were countered with the argument that all the minor showrooms were managed by women while the larger ones had male managers. As there are more female managers than male ones it must follow that in most of the grades the number of women will be greater, but taking the most senior Grade SA/B the nationwide figures are 11 men and nine female – as near parity as one could hope for. As far as Essex is concerned in July 1981 the figures for SA/B establishments were 4 male and 1 female but in March, Basildon was being managed by a woman so that the figures then were two women and three men; again very close to parity . . .

> The applicant produced no factual evidence at all to show that there was even a suggestion of a general policy of sex discrimination and having regard to the figures which we have just quoted, and which were not challenged, we find the suggestion that there is general or local policy of sex discrimination wholly untenable and indeed somewhat unworthy. *(Mrs Whitt v British Gas Corporation)*

Apparently, the tribunal either ignored or failed to grasp the argument that, relative to what one might expect, *comparatively* fewer women than men were promoted from junior management to senior management. The tribunal failed to see that in this situation, 'parity', i.e., equality or near equality in numbers, might well *not* mean that sex discrimination had not occurred. This is not to say that the numbers as quoted in the decision *prove* that sex discrimination *had* occurred: a far closer analysis of the qualifications required, applications received and the selection process would be necessary to support such a finding. The tribunal does not, however, dismiss the evidence on this ground. It merely says that 'near parity' of numbers – a characterisation itself open to question – *suggests* there was no sex discrimination. It does not ask whether women and men *similarly* qualified were receiving equal treatment in promotions. That the tribunal failed to appreciate the complainant's argument seems particuarly likely in view of its characterisation of the complainant's allegation of a discriminatory policy as 'wholly untenable and indeed somewhat unworthy'. In addition, the tribunal's statement that the complainant 'produced no factual evidence at all' is troublesome. First, it is incorrect, as the complainant *had* produced factual evidence (it was *circumstantial* and not *direct* evidence but it was no less factual for that). Secondly, the error suggests a disturbing lack of appreciation of the fact that discrimination of the sort alleged in this case is rarely proven by direct evidence; it is precisely from such circumstantial evidence that it is so often necessary to infer that sex discrimination has occurred.

Frequency of Error

This failure to use the 'comparative' standard applicable to most sex discrimination cases appeared to be fairly frequent. In cases such as those quoted, the tribunal's decision makes the error plain. Also, of the 129 cases in 1980-1982 in which comparative treatment was the issue, 58 decisions did not state the facts of a 'comparator's' situation or treatment. While it is possible that those facts were considered by the tribunals but were simply not mentioned in the decisions, this seems unlikely if the tribunals understood that comparison was central to the case.

Discrimination in Dismissal, Unfair Dismissal, and Redundancy

A number of the decisions where an incorrect standard was used concerned claims about dismissal and, in dismissal cases where complainants claimed their dismissal had been both unfair and discriminatory, it was not uncommon for decisions to state the 'reasonableness' standard on an unfair dismissal claim but to state no different standard for a claim of sex discrimination. A number of decisions certainly gave no indication that any different approach or analysis was made in deciding a discrimination claim. It seems likely that tribunals were in many instances applying the standard used in unfair dismissal and redundancy claims to discrimination claims as well.

Insufficient Analysis of Employers' Explanations

In early cases under the equality legislation[9] the EAT had ruled that, although the formal burden of proof rested with the complainant, in the course of a case, after production of certain evidence by the complainant, the evidential burden might shift to the respondent, who would then have to discharge it.[10] This was similar to the established procedure for discrimination cases in the American courts.[11]

In 1981, however, the EAT appeared to alter the type of analysis expected from industrial tribunals in discrimination cases.[12] In *Khanna*, the tribunals were urged to ignore what the EAT saw as the complexities of the concept of 'burden of proof', and were directed instead simply to:

> . . . take into account the fact that direct evidence of discrimination is seldom going to be available and that, accordingly, in these cases the affirmative evidence of discrimination will normally consist of inferences to be drawn from primary facts. If the primary facts indicate that there has been discrimination of some kind, the employer is called on to give an explanation, and, failing clear and specific explanation being given by the employer to the satisfaction of the industrial tribunal, an inference of unlawful discrimination from the primary facts will mean the complainant succeeds.[13]

The EAT did not, however, discuss specifically what a 'clear and specific explanation' might mean. Although the EAT's intention was obviously to maintain a relatively informal approach in the industrial tribunals by directing them to avoid what it saw as complicated 'legalisms', its *Khanna* instructions – or lack of them – have been criticised as implicitly weakening tribunals' analytical discipline when considering respondents' explanations in equal rights cases.[14] For the purposes of this study the change makes little difference, since many of the decisions reviewed appeared to fall short even of the directions articulated in *Khanna*. In fact, one of the more striking characteristics of the 215 full decisions reviewed was the frequency with which the tribunals based findings of non-discrimination on vague and generalised explanations from respondents, ignoring noted inconsistencies and even accepting as proof of non-discrimination, evidence which was irrelevant to the issues presented. The decisions often rely heavily upon general impressions of the honesty or sincerity of respondents and their witnesses, rather than upon an analysis of the evidence.

Care must be taken in analysing a written decision as a reflection of the hearing it records. To avoid unjustified criticism consideration was given only to those decisions which clearly stated the basis of the tribunal's analysis and not those in which doubts might be due simply to omissions of detail.

Acceptance of Inadequate Explanations

In a number of decisions, tribunals accepted explanations from employers which were vague, or involved obvious inconsistencies which were not resolved, and accepted explanations which were irrelevant or unsupported by any objective or documentary evidence.

In one such case a woman with a successful record of arduous work in the construction industry, was hired by a site foreman. Before she could begin work, his decision to employ her was countermanded by his employer on the grounds that:

(1) he had never employed a woman in 30 years of business;

(2) he felt the site conditions in winter were too hard for a woman; and

(3) he felt the toilet facilities (a single outdoor toilet) were inadequate.

After press and radio coverage of his decision, the employer had relented. The complainant was re-hired, only to be dismissed by the foreman shortly after she began work. The woman filed a case claiming she had been fired the second time because she was a woman. The tribunal decided that she had been fired for lack of ability. In doing so, it accepted the foreman's explanation that he 'could decide quickly whether a person could manage the job'. The tribunal said:

> We also accepted that, in view of the time limit set for this contract, if (the site foreman) could have used the applicant's services he would only have been too glad to do so because of the difficulty he was having in the recruiting of capable building labourers to work on the job which had a tight time schedule . . . (Miss O'Hagan v H Diamond Construction Ltd)

This explanation is certainly suspect in light of the owner's attitude toward women workers and his specific actions with respect to this particular complainant. However, the possibility of any connection between that and the dismissal was simply not commented upon, much less analysed.

In another case the complainant was a woman employed for about two years by the respondents, whose shops both rented and sold televisions and other electrical goods. Her official status was 'sales assistant,' yet for much of the two years she was in sole charge of one of the shops. When the respondents hired new managers for their shops she was not given the opportunity to apply for such a position. (The tribunal decision is no more specific than this.) The complainant filed two claims: one for pay equal to that of one of the male shop managers for the period during which she had had similar responsibilities, and another claiming that the refusal to allow her to apply for a manager's position was discrimination on the grounds of her sex. The tribunal awarded her equal pay. With respect to her sex discrimination claim, it said:

> She did not have expertise in shop management. She had no knowledge of the technicalities of television and electrical instruments. She did not have the years of experience behind her which those who were appointed managers had. Finally, she was unable to drive a motor vehicle. . . . With regard to technical knowledge, we accept that managers really do not require very much: but we are satisfied that the applicant did not have the other qualifications mentioned which management required in appointing a manager of their shops. *(Miss Vickers v N W Electronics (Bradford) Ltd)*

Parts of this analysis ignore quite contrary evidence noted by the tribunal in the decision. The tribunal accepted the employers' statement that the complainant did not have expertise in shop management. Yet she had been left in charge of a shop for a 12 month period – as the tribunal itself recognised in granting her claim for equal pay with another shop manager for this period! As to her alleged lack of technical knowledge, the tribunal stated 'with regard to technical knowledge, we accept that managers really do not require very much . . .' Furthermore, the decision records no evidence about the alleged requirement that a shop manager hold a licence to drive a car. Clearly the complainant had served as a manager for a year without one. This is not to say that the complainant's case *was* proved, although it certainly describes a situation which called for further scrutiny of the employers' alleged reasons for not allowing the complainant to apply for the position. The fact that all of the new managers selected were male and that the complainant was held to have been discriminated against in her wages for over a year, would seem to have emphasised the need to be particularly careful when reviewing the employers' explanations in this case.

In another equal pay case, a male clerical assistant and printer who worked at night claimed equal pay with a woman in a similar position who worked during the day. The history of the man's claim was described by the tribunal:

> In February 1981 he complained to the respondents that his pay was not on par with that of Mrs Wallace who was doing identical work to him. The difference in pay was conceded but it was pointed out that Mrs Wallace's pay was higher than his as a result of her higher grading and the fact that she had merit pay and length of service. *(George Pupkis v British Aerospace PLC)*

Subsequently Mrs Wallace left and was replaced by a Mrs Larcombe, who received the same wages as her predecessor. The tribunal noted that it was 'accepted for all practical purposes that her job is the same as that performed by Mrs Wallace previously'. At the tribunal hearing however, the employers made no reference to 'merit pay' nor to 'length of service' when justifying the pay difference, developing instead a picture of the jobs as being very different. Surely a complete change in an employer's stated reasons for paying different wages should require an explanation. Nevertheless, this tribunal apparently ignored the difference in explanations given to the complainant on the two different occasions. Even though the employer conceded the jobs were identical in some respects, the tribunal simply accepted the respondent's position that the complainant's colleague had additional tasks which constituted a material difference and dismissed the application.

In a few cases, tribunals accepted as 'explanations' of the employer's actions, evidence which itself actually suggested the possibility of discrimination! For example: where a woman alleged several instances of sex discrimination in her employment arrangements, the employer attempted to justify the differences by describing her job as 'supervisory' rather than truly 'managerial'. With respect to the fact that the complainant received significantly less money than the others whom she claimed had similar responsibilities, the tribunal stated:

> It is significant that in her remuneration package, her salary is about £4,500 per annum. The people (men) in Exhibit R/l start their basic salary at about £6,000, which was some indication of the worth that the respondents attach to the functions of the different persons doing managerial with those having supervisory functions. *(Mrs Clarke v Allen Yanis Tipton Ltd)*

Here, the tribunal appears to have assumed the very issue it was to decide. Surely, in a case alleging discriminatory differences in various employment benefits, a difference in salary is *itself* a matter to be investigated rather than accepted automatically as an indication of relative worth.

Similarly, in a case where a female teacher claimed sex discrimination in the selection of a man for promotion to a Deputy Head post, she introduced charts at the hearing to attempt to show a history of preference on the part of senior management for filling senior posts with men. The tribunal commented:

> We remain unconvinced. Of course the figures show a preponderance of male promotions. There were many more males on the staff and many more male applicants for each post. *(Mrs Mason v Coventry City Council)*

Where sex discrimination is alleged, it would seem that a preponderance of male staff, male applications for promotions and male promotion might well suggest a situation which warranted careful and thorough investigation. But for this tribunal the information *defeated* the complainant's case.

Frequency of the Problem

The respondents in these cases appear to have given explanations of their conduct which were less than 'clear and specific,' yet all of them were accepted by the tribunals and the complainant's cases dismissed. Moreover, this was not uncommon: almost one-third of the 215 case decisions reviewed recorded analyses of this type.

Instances of Careful Analysis

There were several tribunal decisions which reflected extremely careful analysis of evidence. However, these tended repeatedly to come from the same few chairman. It is also worth noting that in most of these cases complainants were legally represented by experienced barristers and solicitors, several of whom received EOC support and advice. Examples of such analysis include the following cases:

An employer dismissed two women estate agents despite excellent job performances. The manager responsible justified their dismissal on the grounds that the women were not 'aggressive' sales-persons. To support this allegation, he submitted his assessments of individuals he had interviewed and hired while the complainants were still at the firm. The tribunal said of these documents:

We have not been favourably impressed by this bundle of documentation. In the course of the tribunal's discussions one of my colleagues referred to it as a lot of red herrings. Mr Symonds's assessment of interviewees could only have been of value to us if he had made a similar assessment of the two applicants. He made this assessment of entire newcomers; it would have been easy for him to make a similar assessment of two people already in the employment of the respondents. He was asked by the tribunal if he could produce any similar assessment of the applicants, and he could not. Therefore we discount the alleged importance of these documents which he has put in evidence. *(Mrs Posnette and Mrs Shingler v Barratt Developments)*

The tribunal ultimately found that sex discrimination had occurred and awarded damages.

In a case where a woman alleged discrimination in promotion, the respondents attempted to justify promoting a male 'buyer', with less experience and no better performance record than the complainant, by saying that the complainant's earlier annual assessments had been 'boosted' in order to encourage her. The tribunal did not accept this explanation. It said:

A perusal of those appraisals encourages the belief that both the applicant and Mr Thompson are high flyers. Certainly they are both well above average.

. . . Our suspicions were considerably aroused when in evidence Mr Roberts sought to nullify the applicant's apparent superiority on paper by testifying to the effect that he had boosted his appraisal of her beyond what was fully justified in order to encourage her. We could not understand his alleged reason for doing such a thing in her case but not in that of Mr Thompson. It is our belief that with his lesser experience and shorter period with the Company it is Mr Thompson and not the applicant who would more likely have benefitted from such a boost and falsification of the picture. We believe and find that the appraisal by Mr Roberts of the applicant represented his true opinion of her qualities at the time. *(Mrs Crocker v J C Bamford Excavators Ltd)*

In another case, a woman office manager for an electrical wholesalers claimed she had been selected for redundancy, rather than a man who had been with the firm for only one month, solely because she was a woman. The respondents claimed they kept the man because he would be best able physically to do the job as it was then and 'as it was hoped it would become with the advent of more large deliveries in containers'. They claimed he was needed to do any necessary physical handling in the warehouse in the absence of the two other male members of staff.

On the basis of the testimony presented at the hearing, however, the tribunal rejected this explanation: It said:

> Because she was a woman the company assumed that she did not have the necessary physical strength, an assumption which is manifest from the company's failure to ask if she would be prepared to do occasional physical work in the warehouse and its failure to offer her suitable instruction and a trial to see if she could do such work. In the case of Mr O'Shea, the company made the opposite assumption, that because he is a man he did have the necessary physical strength. Further, the branch's van is normally driven by Mr Baptist but Mr Gallagher has to drive if Mr Baptist is absent or if a second van is hired for a few days to clear the backlog of work. There is also a youth employed in the warehouse, and the occasions when Mr Baptist, Mr Gallagher and Mr Graham would all be unavailable, so that Mrs Kerr would have had to help in the warehouse, would have been very infrequent, as is shown by the experience of Mr O'Shea since Mrs Kerr's dismissal. Mr Rennie argued that it is not sex discrimination to say that one employee is less able to handle heavy items than another employee, but that argument we reject because the basis of selection used by the company was sex and none other. *(Miss Kerr v Clyde Factors Electrical Ltd)*

The tribunal found both sex discrimination *and* unfair dismissal.

Relying upon Subjective or Irrelevant Evidence

As early as 1979, the Court of Appeal made it clear that benevolent motive would not be a defence to complaints of sex discrimination.[15] There did not need to be a *conscious* element in sex discrimination at all.[16] The EAT has held to this position, reversing two tribunal decisions on sex discrimination cases since 1979.[17] In one, the EAT said:

> Those would have been unimpeachable findings [by the industrial tribunal] if the law of sex discrimination in an employment context had been based, like that for example of

unfair dismissal, upon the application to particular circumstances of criteria of reasonableness or fairness; or had depended upon the state of mind or intentions of a particular employer. As it is, however, the whole tenor of the sections of the Act applying to an employment context is to disregard the motive for reasonableness (or otherwise), or degree, or quality of discrimination and to concentrate upon the bare factual question whether discrimination has in fact occurred. We do not think that any of these findings show an appreciation of that distinction . . . A number of the findings indicate, moreover, a preoccupation on the part of the tribunal with topics irrelevant to the issue of sex discrimination – such as the offer of alternative employment, or Miss Creagh's apparently casual attitude to completion of the application form.[18]

Nonetheless, in the decisions reviewed, tribunals frequently expressed concern with respondents' motives, 'intentions', 'honesty' and generosity, and with complainants' 'objectives' and behaviour.

Respondents' Intentions and Honesty

In dismissing an application alleging discriminatory selection for redundancy, one tribunal wrote:

It was suggested by the applicant that the selection was made on the ground of sex discrimination. That was vigorously denied by both Mrs Burton, Mr Peacock and Miss Walsh, the Personnel Director. It is true that before the respondents acquired the business in 1976 there may have been as many as 15 women employed in a semi-skilled capacity. During the period the respondents have run the business the number has probably not exceeded five. Then one of the five left for some reason, leaving four and gradually the numbers have diminished until there are none there now. We have been invited to draw the inference and conclude that the respondents have wanted to get rid of all the women in their workforce. There was no direct evidence to support the suggestion. We have to make up our minds whether we think that Mr Burton and Mr Peacock were honest witnesses or whether we think they were disingenuous. We have no hesitation in coming to the conclusion that they were both honest men and we accept that there was no question here of them selecting the applicant because she was a woman. *(Mrs Louise Jones v Frederick Sage and Co Ltd)*

Another good example of the significance tribunals attached to employers' intentions is the case referred to above (see p.31); despite the fact that discrimination clearly had occurred, the tribunal dismissed the application on the grounds that 'no discrimination was intended' *(Mrs Newman v Alistair Black Ltd)*. Furthermore, in several decisions tribunals noted that the complainant had been 'generously' treated by the respondent. Comments of this sort were not infrequent in tribunal decisions. Forty-five of the 215 decisions reviewed referred to the good intentions of the respondents or to their 'generous treatment' of the complainant (17 of these cases included a claim of unfair dismissal, to which such considerations might be thought to be relevant). Such considerations do not *necessarily* mean a tribunal has mis-applied the law. They do, however, suggest that a tribunal may have been distracted from the proper issues in a case. It does indeed seem that such considerations may well have affected the tribunals' decisions: in 34 of the 45 cases in which such comments were made, the employers won.

Complainants' Objectives or Behaviour

Similarly, a number of tribunals expressed concern with another matter generally irrelevant to an equal pay or sex discrimination claim: the complainant's 'objective' in bringing the claim. This is illustrated by the following statement:

> The applicant says she first raised the matter in October 1981 when she discovered Mr Beahan was receiving approximately £4,300 per annum as against her £3,400 per annum. The memorandum she wrote at that time however refers to 'inequalities of pay amongst the office staff' and makes comparisons with two ladies previously employed as programmers as well as two men and three or four women 'performing almost identical tasks but for totally dissimilar rates of pay.' The objective is (as the memo indicates) to secure a general upgrading of the jobs in the Costing Office and thus remove inequalities although the applicant writes, "it is appreciated that the differentials now seen as inequalities may have been justified when instituted . . ." The applicant was originally trying to obtain a job evaluation review of her department and although in a notice dated 28 October she changed her complaint to a personal basis, that is really her objective. *(Mrs Elliot v Brown and Sharpe Ltd)*

Thirty-four of the 215 decisions expressed concern with complainants' behaviour towards the respondents, the behaviour noted often being characterised as 'antagonistic' or 'ungrateful'. While the fact that the tribunal noted a complainant's behaviour does not necessarily mean that this figured prominently in its analysis, the case results suggest such consideration did have some impact: of the 34 decisions that mentioned complainants' behaviour, complainants lost 30 (11 of the 34 cases included a claim of unfair dismissal, to which a complainant's behaviour might be considered relevant).

Credibility of the Parties

In the 213 decisions from 1980-1982 where facts were in dispute, the tribunals referred to credibility in 67% of the sex discrimination cases and in 39% of the equal pay cases. Among the sex discrimination cases, credibility was mentioned in 52% of the cases concerning dismissal; 80% of the cases concerning recruitment; and 85% of the cases concerning promotion. Credibility is mentioned just as frequently in decisions which referred to documentary evidence as in those which mention only testimonial evidence. In fact, references to credibility were more frequent the greater the amount of documentary information available.

Table 2.1   *Tribunal references to credibility and type of evidence presented, SDA and EQPA hearings, 1980-1982*

	Total cases	Decisions which mention credibility
Facts agreed	2	0
Testimony only	58	31 (53%)
Testimony and existing documents (few)	70	33 (47%)
Testimony and existing documents (several)	35	23 (66%)
Testimony and prepared documents	24	15 (62%)
Testimony and further and better particulars, experts, site visits	26	20 (77%)

The Basis for Assessing Credibility

Half of the tribunal decisions which included findings on credibility made them without explanation. Though there had been a conflict in the evidence, they merely state 'we accept that . . .', 'we are satisfied that . . .'. Over one-third of all the cases which made findings on credibility explained their decisions *not* with respect to other evidence in the case, but simply on the basis of personal reactions to the witness, or to the manner in which they gave their testimony, with statements such as:

We formed a most favourable impression of Mr Scholfield – we accept that on making any recommendations he was influenced solely by the suitability of a candidate for reasons in no way influenced by the candidate's sex or marital status. *(Mrs Stott v Manchester City Council)*

We are satisfied that Mr Pike and Mr Andrews, and in particular the former, were extremely experienced interviewers with a deep and detailed knowledge of the respondents' needs and of the various qualities the work required . . . We accept both witnesses as men of honesty and integrity who held nothing back and who, quite genuinely, formed and held the views they have expressed to us. *(Misses Cropper, Stephens, Drew, Woods and Cahill v The South Western Electricity Board)*

We have been invited to draw the inference and conclude that the respondents have wanted to get rid of all the women in their workforce. There was no direct evidence to support the suggestion. We have to make up our minds whether we think they were disingenuous. We have no hesitation in coming to the conclusion that they were both honest men and we accept that there was no question here of them selecting the applicant because she was a woman. *(Mrs Louise Jones v Frederick Sage and Co Ltd)*

In contrast, there were tribunals, though far fewer in number, which gave very careful analyses of their decisions on credibility, relating their judgements to other evidence before the tribunal. The following are examples.

Mr Shirley said in evidence that he would have treated a man with young children identically with a woman by writing the same letter but in the masculine gender. He testified 'I would have said he should be at home with his children at tea-time as a father . . . I would have said as a father it would have put too much pressure on a wife and family and suggested he got a job nearer to home'. There are very strong grounds for treating that evidence with considerable scepticism and as an afterthought. It is inconsistent with the express terms of the letter of 11 March which refers to a 'young mum with three kiddies' and also with the lengthy letter of 28 April, in particular the third full paragraph on page 3 (Exhibit R11 also A9) in which *inter alia* Mr Shirley states: 'Young children need a mother's attention, especially when schooling commences' *(Mrs Shirley Ali Khan v Kent Country Nurseries Ltd)*.

On Monday 7 June Miss Brennan went to the Union Street shop and saw Mr French. Her evidence as to what took place in that interview was almost exactly the same as the written statement she submitted with her application to the tribunal and we therefore do not repeat it. Mr French gave a different account of the interview. We have no hesitation in preferring Miss Brennan's version of what took place. Mr French's evidence was wholly unconvincing and was in conflict with the statement submitted with the Notice of Appearance which was based on information supplied by him, and with the particulars supplied to the applicant's solicitor on 3 November *(Miss Brennan v (1) J H Dewhurst Ltd and (2) Mrs D M French)*.

Not without hesitation, we are not satisfied that Mr Sutherland was promoted to office manager. We are satisfied that he was employed as a sales negotiator. We appreciate when we come to this finding it is contrary to the direct evidence of three persons, two of whom are partners, and as I have stated one of them was called as a witness for the applicant. However, against that there is the letter to Mr Sutherland giving him the salary increase. We find it surprising, indeed very surprising, that if he was being promoted to the office manager that there would be no reference to this in the letter. Surely, one would expect some reference to a promotion with an increase in salary. There is also the fact that we accept the evidence of Miss Day that she knew nothing of such a promotion. There were only the two of them in the office, that is Mr Sutherland and Miss Day. Surely if he had been promoted with additional responsibility she would have known about it. Furthermore, one would have thought that if he had been promoted to office manager there would have been some contemporaneous documentary support for this; perhaps it would have been in a memo; perhaps it would have been in a minute of a partners' meeting, when the promotion was decided upon. One would have thought there would be something available. In fact, nothing has been put forward by the respondents to support this. The only document is very much against them, namely, the letter to which I have already referred, and contemporaneous documents when there are disputes over the evidence are very helpful *(Mrs Moghadam v Amos Horsburgh & Partners)*.

Excessive Reliance upon Credibility

It is of course common sense to expect that credible witnesses should tend to increase a party's chance of success. The major importance credibility plays in tribunals' decisions on sex discrimination and equal pay claims is, however, cause for some concern. First, and most obviously, it presents the possibility that the subjective, 'personal' question of credibility will allow fuller play to personal biases or preferences than would more objective grounds of decision. Secondly, it may mean that certain considerations which are often not proper in discrimination and equal pay cases may in fact be being used to decide them, e.g. good intentions, genuine belief. It must also be said that in the legal world of appellate review 'credibility covers a multitude of errors'. Chairmen – and, by now, surely tribunal members – are aware that a finding of credibility will rarely be disturbed by the higher courts and – consciously or unconsciously – may be tempted to use credibility to explain decisions for that reason. A third concern about the frequency with which decisions refer to credibility is therefore that this may effectively isolate a substantial number of decisions from meaningful appellate review. A fourth concern has been voiced by experts on discrimination law in Britain: that findings on an individual's honesty or truthfulness ignore the fact that people are not always aware of their own prejudices and motivations. Noting several racial discrimination cases in which credibility was a major factor, one authority stated:

> It is obviously unsatisfactory to allow subjective evidence of a racial ground to be rebutted by the evidence of the very person or persons whose state of mind is in question. The tribunals . . . have undoubtedly made an effort to evaluate the credibility of such self-serving and uncheckable evidence, but merely to conclude that the witness is honest takes no account of the fact that people are not always aware of their own prejudices and motivations.[19]

Another solicitor, experienced with sex discrimination claims, has written specifically of the:

> difficulties of persuading tribunals to draw the appropriate inferences on the surrounding circumstances and not to accept the subjective views of the person making the personal decision, however truthful that person is, without objective evidence to support the defence being put forward. It would appear that at present tribunals do not look for the objective evidence to support a respondent's claim . . .[20]

50

Certainly in the period covered by this study, this appeared to be true. Tribunals appeared to rely heavily and frequently upon impressions of parties' credibility without making full use of available documentary evidence.

Lack of Uniformity in Tribunal Decisions

There is considerable lack of uniformity among tribunals on the substantive issues which appear frequently in sex discrimination and equal pay cases. This section presents representative excerpts from decisions on a number of such issues, including: the relevance of past discrimination by a respondent; the significance of evidence of general non-discrimination; issues important in claims of discrimination in promotion; 'justifiable' indirect discrimination; and 'material difference,' 'like work,' and other issues in equal pay claims.

Tribunals also differed in their approach to two matters of particular importance in sex discrimination cases: compensation for loss of employment opportunity and for injury to feelings, and the significance of employers' answers to s.74 questionnaires. The section also includes detailed discussions of these topics.

The Relevance of Past Discrimination

Tribunals expressed quite different attitudes about the value of evidence concerning an employer's discriminatory acts which were, at the time of the hearing, 'out-of-time': some viewed them as providing illuminating historical background; others dismissed them as utterly irrelevant. In one such case several women claimed both direct and indirect discrimination in their selection for redundancy. The tribunal rejected this claim, although it did note the traditional male-female job demarcations at the respondent's factory and examined the situation in detail, stating:

> The claims under the SDA are of unlawful discrimination in respect of the selection for redundancy. Any claims arising out of any unlawful discrimination there may have been in the past relating to recruitment and development of labour would be well out of time. Nevertheless the historical background is very relevant in this, as often in other, sex discrimination cases. *(Mrs Grace (and seven others) v Kraft Foods Ltd)*

In a different case, a self-represented complainant alleged sex discrimination in promotion, a claim which directly implicated the headmaster of the school where she taught. She used other teachers from her school as witnesses, one of whom testified that, in previous years, other women teachers in the school had complained of discriminatory treatment by the same headmaster. No doubt these complaints were strictly out of time with respect to the current case, but the vehemence of the tribunal's reaction went beyond that; it said:

> Not only is the period thereby defined when those complaints arose (the precise dates were not given to us) but the 'complaints' (described in a most brief generalised fashion) do not appear (at least so far as two of them are concerned) to have been referred at any time to the Headmaster. It is a complete waste of time to put before us matters of trivia of this nature. *(Mrs Stott v Manchester City Council)*

Evidence of General Non-Discrimination

Several tribunals accepted sparse, uncorroborated, and even irrelevant evidence as proof that the respondents did not generally discriminate against women in promotion, accepting that evidence as defeating the particular claim of discrimination they were hearing. For example, in one case, the complainant claimed that she had been treated less favourably than men on the staff both by the respondents generally and specifically by her own supervisor (another woman). The tribunal found that the supervisor had not discriminated. It also found the employers had not discriminated, reasoning that the fact that the supervisor, a woman, had been promoted, indicated that 'there is no policy in the respondents of sex discrimination'! *(Pamela Darlowe v (1) Plessey Connectors Ltd, (2) Plessey Management Services Ltd, (3) Mrs H Coley).*

In another case, a different tribunal commented on the significance of similar evidence more appropriately:

> Mrs Davies put forward an analysis of the number of female caretakers and assistant caretakers in the County which clearly indicates that the respondents do appoint women to these positions. The production of this evidence does not of itself discharge the burden of proof. Of course, had the document disclosed that there were no women at all in these positions it would have strengthened the hand of the applicant. As it is, it still leaves open the question as to whether, in particular circumstances when a particular Board of Governors was making a particular appointment, an act of sex discrimination took place. *(Sarah Davies v Durham County Council)*

Sex Discrimination in Promotion

A significant proportion of sex discrimination claims by women involve allegations of discrimination in promotion. Decisions on this issue differ very markedly both with regard to the issues identified for consideration and in the thoroughness with which these are considered. The following are two examples:

Deviation from an Established Promotion Procedure

In a situation involving a respondent with 'an excellent system of staff appraisal', a tribunal found it significant that solely for the purposes of this complainant's promotion, a special selection board had been set up to handle interviews. It explained:

> Of great concern in our estimation is the setting up of an ad hoc selection board to interview the three candidates. Such a procedure was wholly exceptional. The ordinary procedure would have been for Mr Roberts to reach a conclusion on his own and for Mr Coyne, the purchasing director, to have confirmed Mr Robert's choice unless Mr Coyne felt there were exceptional circumstances. It is said on behalf of the respondents that there were exceptional circumstances in this case, but the remainder of our reasons will demonstrate why we do not accept that . . .

> By the end of the hearing we were all convinced that had the applicant been a man there would have been no question of setting up the selection board. The applicant would have been appointed. She had very nearly double the experience of Mr Thompson. In Mr Robert's estimation, at the end of 1979, she as well as Mr Thompson was capable of much higher responsibility. The applicant was scored as being outstanding in two respects – Mr Thompson in none. Mr Roberts reported the applicant to have been very good under four heads and Mr Thompson under only three. *(Mrs Crocker v J C Bamford Excavators Ltd)*

In another promotion case before a different tribunal, a similar variation in normal procedure was treated very lightly. A woman second deputy head, not selected for first deputy head, alleged that the selection of the male third deputy head for the post had been discriminatory. With respect to the change in the selection process, the tribunal noted simply:

Thereafter the three deputy heads were interviewed by a committee of three governors who then decided upon the person to become first deputy head . . . The three deputy heads were interviewed being asked similar questions, then the governors deliberated to decide whom to appoint with the advisers present but not voting . . . Apparently this procedure had not been used before at Hadfield and though there may have been occasions when a second deputy head moved up to first without interview, the Tribunal was satisfied that the procedure was one the governors were entitled to adopt and reasonable in the circumstances. *(Vera Gould v Derbyshire County Council)*

The decision provides no further details. It is to be noted that the complainant's solicitor who had filed the application out of time, apparently did not argue that this process was unfair.

Discriminatory Questions at Interviews

An unsatisfactory performance at an interview is often a reason given by an employer to justify the decision not to promote the complainant. Some tribunals specifically acknowledged that the discriminatory use of certain questions during such an interview could seriously affect a complainant and/or their performance; others ignored this possibility entirely. In one case where an interviewer had asked the complainant questions about 'whether she intended to have a family in the near future, and what were her relations with her husband', the complainant claimed these questions upset her and negatively influenced her performance at the interview. The tribunal stated:

Miss Gates says that she was upset by those questions and we accept that this was so, though all the evidence indicates that she did not show it. It indicates rather that she answered the offending questions calmly and appeared to take them in her stride. Miss Taylor told us that she was surprised that Miss Gates appeared not to be ruffled by them, and that she answered them calmly. This of itself tends to show that the questions and the way they were put were such that they might well be objectionable to and upset a woman in Miss Gates' position. Our colleague Mrs McQuaid, with long relevant experience says, and we accept from her, that in such circumstances a woman of experience and intelligence may well control her reactions and remain cool but the effect of such question and the resulting upset will be there nevertheless. We are all satisfied that Miss Gates' apparent lack of adverse reaction probably required an effort on her part and would probably make her less relaxed and more guarded in the way in which she dealt with the remainder of the interview. *(Miss Gates v Wirral Borough Council)*

In another case, where a woman failed to win promotion to senior buyer within a firm, the respondents maintained the male applicant was selected largely because he 'gave a much better account of himself before the committee than did the applicant'. The tribunal found, however, that this was explained by the interviewing board's own attitude and the complainant's response to it:

> If then the applicant gave the impression, when interviewed by the board, that she was less enthusiastic than Mr Thompson, as is alleged, we are fully satisified that she has rightly identified the reason for it. We accept her evidence that the board was overly concerned about her intentions and those of her husband in relation to the likelihood of his continuing to work abroad. The applicant complains that the first half at least of the interview was devoted to that and like topics, which were given complete precedence over her general suitability and competence for the job. *(Mrs Crocker v J C Bamford Excavators Ltd)*

Yet in another case, a tribunal accepted that the respondents rejected the complainant for a position because she was 'abrasive' at an interview, disregarding the facts that suggested this may have been in response to the interviewers' own attitudes and behaviour. The complainant alleged she was rejected for promotion to a position as timekeeper because she was a woman. She had done better on the aptitude test than any other candidates; the respondents blamed her performance at her interview at which, her two interviewers said, she had been 'aggressive and abrasive'. The interviewers' own behaviour at the interview was quite extraordinary: they tried to dissuade her from taking the job, gave her incorrect information about two aspects of it, and then were not 'pleased' when she corrected them. Judging her 'too agressive and abrasive', they did not check with her colleagues to determine whether this was her normal behaviour. In this case, the tribunal held that the interviewers' impression of the complainant was reasonable, despite the fact that they had done nothing to verify their impressions. The tribunal failed even to consider whether the interviewers themselves might have influenced or caused the complainant's reaction *(Mrs Baker v Fairey Engineering Ltd)*.

Justifiable Indirect Discrimination

A requirement or condition which is neutral on its face but which has disproportionate negative impact on individuals of one sex, is said to be 'indirectly' discriminatory and is generally forbidden by the SDA 1975, s.1(1)(b). However, such discrimination is permitted where an employer can show that the requirement or condition is 'justifiable' for reasons unrelated to sex. In spite of attempts by the EAT to offer guidance on this matter, tribunals have taken quite varied attitudes towards the definition of 'justifiability', both in the 'degree' of justification they will require and in the amount of evidence they demand of parties attempting to establish (or refute) justifiability. Two cases which considered claims of indirect discrimination in selection for redundancy are illustrative. In each, women claimed that the retention of skilled workers was indirectly discriminatory. Neither tribunal ultimately found the retention of skilled workers unjustifiable, but their approaches to this question and the tenor of their decisions were distinctly different – one taking quite a close look at the proffered justification, the other barely reviewing the question. The first stated:

> We are satisfied that the ongoing needs of the business undoubtedly required employees with the maximum versatility and experience to meet changing needs and changing production methods. This was a matter not merely of business convenience but in the existing and anticipated circumstances, of economic necessity. It was a condition for retention of employees which was justifiable. Those least suitable for the ongoing needs of the business were those employees who had only limited experience; mainly on the production line.

This tribunal did however specifically note that it had not been shown that the fact so many women were unskilled in this area was due to any past discrimination by the employers, adding this precautionary note:

> If a traditional attitude amongst the workforce, acquiesced in and probably found convenient by management, results in a demarcation of jobs which closes to even the few women willing and able to do them, jobs which offer more scope for versatility of training and experience, and therefore better employment prospects, that is in our view direct discrimination against women. There is no evidence that any of the

present applicants fall into that category; but that past discrimination tainted, at least potentially, the eventual redundancy situation even if it did not cause the selection for redundancy of any particular woman. *(Mrs Grace (and seven others) v Kraft Foods Ltd)*

The tribunal then proceeded to describe how the employers might approach job recruitment and assignment in the future, to be certain possible discrimination was avoided.

In the second case, the complainants were cabinet shop workers who claimed both unfair selection for redundancy and that the selection was discriminatory. The tribunal in this case merely stated that the use of the criterion 'skilled time served' was not indirect discrimination since, although women could not have met that requirement, it was justifiable 'in so far as it was commercially sound . . .' *(Delia O'Brien v Schreiber Furniture Ltd)*

Equal Pay Claims

Like Work and Material Differences

The EQPA 1970, s.1(2) and (3) provides that individuals will be entitled to equal pay with fellow employees of the other sex where they do 'like work' with no 'material differences'. Quite different views as to what constitutes 'like work' and what differences are sufficiently 'material' to defeat an equal pay claim were taken by different tribunals. Some tribunals took views that appeared to be fairly narrow. One held a woman bingo caller's work was materially different from her male counterpart's because each called different types of bingo games for part of the day and, at the day's end, briefly undertook different tasks to 'complete the day's activities' *(Lucille Goy v Clifton Bingo Club)*. Another denied a female rent and rates rebates officer equal pay with a male rates rebates officer where their work was substantially the same, except that only the woman deputised for her superior during the latter's holidays and only the man completed an annual statistical return on rates rebates for the Department of the Environment *(Mrs Coley v Hinkley and Bosworth Borough Council)*. Other tribunals took a broader view, upholding claims even where there were many differences between the jobs at issue, finding that these were not of practical importance. For example, one tribunal awarded a female bindary assistant, classified as a 'hopper-feeder', equal pay to a male bindary assistant, classified as a 'layer-up', even though they had quite distinct functions and the male layer-up carried a greater load over a larger distance more frequently. It decided these differences were not of practical importance, the need for greater physical strength in the layer-up being counter-balanced by the hopper-feeder's need for greater skill, dexterity and aptitude *(Mrs Nixon v Jarrold and Sons Ltd)*. Another tribunal awarded a female petrol attendant equal pay with her male counterpart, deciding that the fact that the male more frequently took deliveries from tankers and undertook the dipping of petrol tanks did not consititute a material difference in their jobs *(Mrs Wakefield v Newickton Ltd)*. In a separate case involving petrol pump attendants, another tribunal awarded equal pay despite the fact that the woman had no experience working on the forecourt and the male attendants had the tasks of taking weekly dips and receiving tanker loaders *(Mrs Beryl McDade v Bradshaws Motor House Ltd)*.

Separately Paid Tasks

At least two tribunals granted equal pay where the male comparator had some quite different tasks, on the grounds that the different work was compensated for separately. One held there was *no* material difference in the jobs of waitress and waiter, where the waiter was paid separately for work he did from time to time outside his normal working hours *(Mrs Adetti v Linden Hotels Ltd)*. In another case, where a female flying instructor claimed equal pay with a male flying instructor at the same school, the tribunal ordered equal pay even though the male instructor had management responsibilities and did radio navigational work that the woman did not. The tribunal granted the woman pay equal to that *proportion* of the male instructor's wages which was specifically for his work as instructor *(Miss Foye v East Midland School of Flying Ltd)*.

Other tribunals, however, did not use this analysis where it appeared to be eminently appropriate. One considered a man's occasional services as a chauffeur as part of a material difference even though he was paid an additional amount each week for that task *(Lucille Goye v The Clifton Bingo Club)* and another denied a relief branch manager of an insurance company a salary equal to an ordinary branch manager because the ordinary manager had to seek and obtain insurance business even though the ordinary manager received specific *commissions* for her sales *(Mr Dimmer v The Ideal Benefit Society)*.

Grading Systems

A 'material difference' under EQPA 1970, s.1(3) will be found to exist where the difference in pay is due to a grading structure based upon ability, skill, and experience and is fairly applied, irrespective of sex.[21] However, where a tribunal finds elements of discrimination in the practical operation and application of salary scales, s.1(3) will not serve as protection and equal pay will be awarded. In the period studied, decisions by tribunals on applications involving grading systems varied greatly in the extent to which the facts about the application of the system were considered in deciding the case. One tribunal granted equal pay when it found that, although the employer's job assessments were bona fide, the respondent had placed men into higher categories than the female complainants, when in practice, the men did not have the flexibility the assessment assumed *(Mrs McCabe (and seven others) v International Computers Ltd)*. Yet another tribunal rejected an equal pay claim because the respondent set wages by using a grading scheme. The tribunal observed: 'If a man and a woman on the same grade get the same number of points in an appraisal, they would get the same salary'. This decision was in spite of the tribunal accepting evidence that the employers were operating their system of appraisal extremely erratically, with differences in the treatment accorded the complainant as opposed to that accorded a male employee *(Mrs Deignan v Lambeth, Southwark and Lewisham Health Authority)*.

Compensation

Under the SDA 1975 a tribunal may award two distinct types of compensation: compensation for the loss the complainant has incurred as a result of the discrimination, and compensation for injury to her feelings.[22] From 1980-1982, complainants were successful in 41 sex discrimination cases taken to tribunal hearings, with these two types of compensation discussed in just over 30 decisions. In another decision, injury to feelings was not mentioned, even though it seemed appropriate; and in the remaining cases the amount of compensation was left to the parties to agree. With respect to both types of compensation, the tribunals differed both in their approach to the issues presented and in the size of their awards.

Loss of Employment Opportunity

When deciding whether a complainant should receive compensation for loss of employment or loss of employment opportunity, the tribunals appeared generally to apply a test of weighing the probabilities that he or she would have been selected for or continued in the job had the discrimination not occurred. However, their specific applications of this approach were quite diverse, even inconsistent. For example, in one case involving a complainant who was in a field of five or six applicants for a position, the tribunal calculated the compensation due according to the complainant's likelihood of actually obtaining the post.

We were informed that the applicant was unemployed for one week after attending the respondents' shop for the interview and lost the sum of £23.20. He was then engaged under a Job Experience Scheme for three weeks and his loss amounted to £3.35 a week. This is based on the fact that the applicant would have obtained the job with the respondents. It is quite impossible to say whether the applicant would if he had been fairly considered, obtained such employment. We cannot say more than that it was a 50-50 chance and therefore we award the sum of £15 towards the loss he suffered arising out of the possibility that he might have been given the employment by the respondents. *(Mr Anderson v Westbury Radio)*

Another tribunal reasoned differently, feeling it would not award compensation unless it could find the complainant would definitely have obtained the post had it not been for the discrimination. It said:

. . . we find it exceedingly difficult in these circumstances, for us to say on a balance of probabilities that Mr Teader would obtain the post. Had there been but two applicants, including Mr Teader, and there was clear evidence that the existence of Mr Teader would have perhaps made a considerable difference to the company's choice, then we would have found the task easier, but with the best will in the world, where six people are interviewed (with Mr Teader it would have been seven) clearly the odds are stacked against each one person as an individual. In all these circumstances we are quite unable to conclude that on a balance of probabilities Mr Teader would have obtained the post had he not been discriminated against. *(Mr Teader v Hugh Symons & Associates Ltd)*

Another tribunal, which felt the complainant may well have been suitable for the job at issue, rejected the entire concept of compensation for the loss of the job opportunity based upon the probability of his selection.

It seemed to the tribunal that the respondents had been in breach of section 6 of the Sex Discrimination Act 1975 in that they had refused to offer him employment and had made it impossible for him to even have an interview on sexual grounds. Whether or not he was suitable for the job was never considered and on the balance of probabilities he may well have been . . . When it comes to considering compensation the only sensible amount to award in a case of this sort was compensation under the provisions of section 66(4) of the Act, namely compensation for injury to feelings. We are unanimous that the applicant should on this occasion be compensated to the extent of £50. *(Mr O'Connell v Adams Personnel Employment Agency)*

Injury to Feelings

The amounts of money awarded to complainants to compensate for injury to feelings fit no explainable pattern: amounts of £0.50, £7.50, £20, £25, £50, £75, £100, £150, £200 and £1000 were awarded for reasons entirely within the judgement of the individual tribunal hearing the case. Awards described as 'nominal' ranged from £7.50 to £100. Awards for injury to feelings described as 'slight' or 'not severe' ranged from £25 to £50 to £100. There were unexplained awards for amounts of £50, £75 and £100. This lack of consistency was undoubtedly exacerbated by the fact that during the three-year period reviewed, few chairmen decided more than a single case dealing with injury to feelings. A definite observation that can be made, however, is that there was a markedly more restrictive attitude in the tribunals' awards for injury to feelings after the decisions of the EAT and the Court of Appeal in *Coleman v Skyrail Oceanic Ltd.*[23] In that decision the court held an award for £1,000 was excessive for the injury proved, and decreased the amount to £100. Before the *Skyrail* decision, there were several tribunals which had awarded £100 for even 'slight' injury to feelings – where they were awarding 'nominal' damages, or where they were making a modest award to mark the position' *(Mrs Shipston v Gosport Borough Council)*. Since *Skyrail* the amounts have dropped, with several tribunals acknowledging the decision and taking pains to justify even small awards.

> We have been pressed with a submission that damages under this head ought normally to be comparatively small and we were referred to the decision of *Skyrail Oceanic Ltd v Coleman* [1981] ICR 864 as authority for that proposition. We accept their proposition and consider that in this case a nominal sum of £7.50 will suffice for damages under that heading. *(Mr Dwyer v Ciro Pearls Ltd)*

> The applicant has described her feelings as being hurt and shocked by the act of discrimination. She does not suggest, however (and it is plain that this is not the case), that her health has been adversely affected in any way. Accordingly

we are satisfied that a nominal sum for injury to feelings should be awarded of £50. *(Stubbs v Ronald Philip Nathanson t/a Zac's Restaurant)*

We rate the injury to the applicant's feelings to be relatively severe. She is a woman who has committed herself very much to her profession and to a professional life. To her particularly, the questions put by Mr Wilson would be objectionable and to some extent probably distressing – as much, if not more, in retrospect as at the time. What is the appropriate measure of compensation? One cannot put a value on feelings. What we have to try to do is mark our view of the severity of the injury to feelings without being extravagant. We refer to the Court of Appeal's decision in *Coleman v Skyrail Oceanic Ltd* [1981] IRLR 398. An award of £1,000 for injury to feelings was cut down to £100. Mrs Coleman was discriminated against in September 1978. There have been nearly three years of inflation between then and the discrimination against Miss Gates. We consider £100 to be somewhat nominal today and in our view the sum of £200 would be appropriate. *(Miss Gates v Wirral Borough Council)*

Basis for Decisions on Compensation

There were a number of tribunal decisions which did not reveal the nature or the amount of the award for injury to feelings, or even whether an award was actually made. Some decisions stated only a single amount for 'compensation,' without stating whether an award for injury to feelings was included; others stated that an amount had been awarded for injury to feelings but did not state the basis for the award; and where parties agreed an amount of compensation after the tribunal found there had been discrimination, there was usually no indication whether they had included compensation for injury to feelings. This pattern is lamentable. The decisions on compensation are few, and even fewer provide any indication as to the rationale applied by the tribunals. Although such explanation may not be required, it would be of assistance to persons contemplating filing cases, to those advising complainants and respondents (such as ACAS, trades unions, the EOC, the NCCL, and the legal community), as well as those tribunals who will face these issues in the future. This is particularly important in view of the tribunals' frequent tendency to make a finding of discrimination but leave negotiation of the compensation to the parties.

Use of the S.74 Questionnaire

The SDA 1975, s74(1) provides for the use of a form with which individuals who believe they may have been discriminated against on the basis of sex, may question a person on 'his reasons for doing any relevant act, or any other matter, which is or may be relevant' with a view to deciding 'whether to institute proceedings and, if he does so, to formulate and present his case in the most effective manner.' Section 74(2)(b) provides that the questions and replies are admissible in evidence at the tribunal proceedings, and, further, that:

> if it appears to the court or tribunal that the respondent deliberately, and without reasonable excuse, omitted to reply within a reasonable period or that his reply is evasive or equivocal, the . . . tribunal may draw any inference from that fact that it considers is just and equitable to draw, including an inference that he committed an unlawful act.

The procedure was innovative and seemed potentially very advantageous to the sex discrimination complainant. Unfortunately, the tribunal decisions from 1980-1982 indicate that the s.74 questionnaire is actually being used infrequently and on a very limited basis at tribunal hearings. A total of only 16 decisions out of the 215 reviewed mentioned that a section 74 questionnaire had been sent to the respondent; it was mentioned in a further three cases in Scotland. This is a very small number, even assuming that questionnaire responses were produced at some hearings but not mentioned in the decision. Several decisions indicated that the complainant had sent the questionnaire after advice from the EOC.

Evaluating whether and to what extent the questionnaire had been useful to complainants was difficult in several cases since the decisions merely stated that the questionnaire and responses to it were among the documents submitted, but did not indicate what information had been requested or obtained. A few case decisions did describe questionnaire responses, but in an extremely abbreviated form; others rejected the response without explaining their content. None the less a few observations can be made:

In several cases, tribunals did not consider it important that information in the s.74 responses was inaccurate or was contradicted at the hearing. In one case, the tribunal felt inaccuracies in the s.74 reply were simply a genuine mistake due to the passage of time. Another tribunal felt that a questionnaire response which suggested that a potentially discriminatory test had been used, was a matter of oversight, which occurred:

no doubt (because) the Treasury Solicitor was relying on instructions which would have to be obtained rather hurriedly . . . *(Ms Saunders v Manpower Services Commission)*.

The tribunal ruled that the evidence at the hearing overcame the 'unfortunate' questionnaire response.

Difficulties of this sort in using the s.74 procedure have been recognised by commentators.[24]

A few tribunals drew negative inferences from the failure to answer a s.74 questionnaire, but only where the inference was justified by considerable additional evidence. One example involved a case where a woman claimed discrimination in recruitment. The owner of a nursery had refused to consider her application for a job as a grower, stating that a young mother should be looking after her children and would not be able to move to take up the job, an assumption he made without inquiring about the complainant's own circumstances. The employer later justified his refusal with other reasons, but, partly because of his inconsistency and partly because he had failed to reply specifically to the complainant's s.74 questionnaire, the tribunal declined to believe him, drawing the inference that discrimination had occurred *(Mrs Shirley Ali Khan v Kent Country Nurseries Ltd)*.

In another recruitment case, a male telex operator claimed the respondent employment agency had told him a vacancy for a telex operator was with an employer who wished to employ a woman. Two s.74 questionnaires were sent to the respondents, but they failed to reply. This fact may have influenced the tribunal in finding discrimination had occurred, although it was also true that the respondents had not filed a Notice of Appearance and did not attend the hearing, despite the fact that they had discussed the case on the telephone with the complainant, the EOC and the tribunal itself *(Mr O'Connell v Adams Personnel Employment Agency)*.

A few tribunals did rely heavily on the s.74 questionnaire responses in reaching their decisions. In England and Wales, however, only one tribunal relied heavily upon questionnaire responses to decide the crucial issue of a case: whether or not the respondent had stated he wanted to hire only a man. The complainant testified that the manager had explained to her that, as a man had left, they wanted a male replacement to keep the office staff ratio equal.

With respect to the s.74 questionnaire, the tribunal said:

> On the back of that form, the applicant had filled in various questions which she had been advised to pose by the EOC and sent the form to the respondent. That form was duly returned by the respondent, certainly with an answer to the questions referred to in paragraph 5 of the form, but one question was not answered and that was a question which said:
>
> > 'Do you agree that the statement in paragraph 2 is an accurate description of what happened? (i.e. the statement quoted above). If not, in what respect do you disagree or what is your version of what happened?'
>
> In many cases we might not attach any particular importance to the fact that some person had not filled in a form correctly, but here we are dealing with a man, who is a director in an insurance broker's firm and who should be familiar with filling in forms and we think it is of some significance that he did not see fit to deny the allegation which was an allegation of discrimination at that time. We are also impressed by the fact that the applicant is quite adamant that Mr Beckett did make that remark and on balance of probability we have decided that he did and to arrange matters in that way was an unlawful act of discrimination contrary to section 6(1)(a) of the Act. We, therefore, find that the applicant was unlawfully discriminated against. *(Mrs Clark v Elcoates Insurances (Ipswich) Ltd)*

The Effectiveness of the Questions Procedure

Some individuals feel it may be increasingly unrealistic to expect the questionnaire procedure to elicit truly significant information. One commentator has written:

> It is possible that in some instances the employer's replies would furnish the person aggrieved with a basis for a case, especially where the replies were evasive or equivocal, but by and large only the incompetent or unwary employer would disclose anything to his detriment in his replies to a s.74 inquiry.[25]

Furthermore, several lawyers interviewed for this study expressed dissatisfaction with a 'side effect' of the procedure; explaining that the questionnaire provides the respondent with so much information about the claim that it greatly diminishes the possiblity of obtaining spontaneous testimony at a hearing. Nevertheless, some tribunal chairmen believe that the s.74 procedure could fruitfully be used in many more cases. There certainly were cases where the use of a s.74 questionnaire would have assisted greatly by clarifying positions of the parties in advance. Indeed, on a few occasions, tribunals specifically expressed regret that the questionnaire had not been used *(Mrs Humphries v Dunlop Ltd)*. The fact also remains that in a number of the cases reviewed, the questionnaire responses were quite helpful to the complainant in providing the case. None the less, it does seem that to be useful the questions must be drawn effectively, and discrepancies skilfully pursued at the hearing. It also seems clear that questionnaire replies themselves will rarely prove a case – complainants must seek to develop other persuasive evidence to support their allegation if they wish to succeed.

Notes

1   SDA 1975, s.1(1)(b).
2   *Steel v The Post Office* [1978] IRLR 198.
3   SDA 1975, s.7(2)(d) and (e).
4   Under SDA 1975, s.6(2)(a).
5   Under SDA 1975, s.6(2)(b), the tribunal wrote:
    'The applicant, who is still employed by the respondent at the Leigh Showroom, has brought these proceedings under the Sex Discrimination Act 1975, alleging that contrary to the provisions of s.6(2)(a) the respondents discriminated against her in the way they afforded her access to opportunities for promotion – in short, she is saying *that she did not get the job* simply because she was a woman.' *(Mrs Whitt v British Gas Corporation)* (emphasis supplied).
6   On an equal pay application, the complainant acknowledged that there was a grading system but asserted that it was not fairly operated irrespective of sex, relying upon *National Vulcan Engineering Insurance Group Ltd v Wade* [1978] IRLR 225. She pointed to very extraordinary differences in the respondents' appraisals of herself and a male co-worker. But the tribunal said:
    'We reject that submission. We accept the respondents' submission that if a man and a woman on the grade got the same number of points on an appraisal, they would get the same salary. We therefore find that there was no discrimination against Mrs Lewis on the grounds of her sex, and that the respondents were genuinely, if somewhat erratically, operating a grading scheme.' *(Mrs Lewis v SGS Inspection Services Ltd)*
The tribunal thus entirely failed to appreciate the complainant's allegation that there was discrimination *in the appraisals themselves*, the sort of

discrimination envisaged in *National Vulcan*.

7   The tribunal faced the question whether the complainant before it might claim equal pay with her male successor. It acknowledged the decision of the Court of Appeal in *Macarthys Ltd v Smith* [1980] IRLR 210, [1980] ICR 673, which held that a woman could base an equal pay claim on a comparison with her male predecessor, and then said:

> 'The tribunal, had it been necessary, would have found that the applicant could not claim equal pay with a man appointed to her position after she had left, because her successor need not necessarily have been a man and if a woman had been appointed, her salary would have been the same as the man's'. *(D J W Cuthbert v May and Baker Ltd)*

It is difficult to understand precisely what the tribunal did intend, but it does not reflect a clear understanding of the law.

8   For an excellent discussion of the types of comparisons made and the evidentiary difficulties they present, see Bindman (1980) (LSG 77:12).

9   See *Peake v Automative Products* [1978] 1 All ER 106; *Seide v Gillette Industries Ltd* [1980] IRLR 427.

10   *Oxford v DHSS* [1977] ICR 884.

11   See, generally, the discussion in Pannick, (1981).

12   See *Khanna v Ministry of Defence* [1981] ICR 653. The case involved an allegation of racial discrimination, but because of similarities in the legislation the decision applies to sex discrimination cases as well. Its principles would also be applicable to the tribunals' approach to claims for equal pay.

13   *Khanna*, at 658-659.

14   Pannick (1981), p897.

15   *Ministry of Defence v Jeremiah* [1979] 3 All ER 883.

16   Bindman, (1980) (LSG 77:46).

17   In *Creagh v Speedway Sign Service*, Appeal No EAT 312/83 and *Hassan v Harlow District Council and J Ward*, Appeal No EAT 161/84.

18   *Creagh v Speedway Sign Service* Appeal No EAT 312/83.

19   Bindman, (1980) (LSG 77:46).

20   Donnelly (1982).

21   *National Vulcan Engineering Group Ltd v Wade* [1978] IRLR 225.

22   SDA 1975, ss.65,66.

23   [1981] IRLR 398.

24   Lustgarten (1977).

25   Creighton (1979), p215.

CHAPTER 3

EXPLAINING THE PROBLEMS

Why, several years after the SDA 1975 and the EQPA 1970 were enacted, were tribunals still making mistakes in applying certain provisions, especially the basic requirement of equal treatment? Why were they failing to follow the guidance of the EAT in the explanations they expected from employers and in the weight they gave to employers' motives and intentions? Why were they relying so frequently upon judgements of credibility? Observations at hearings and the review of decisions suggest three possible explanations:

(1) that the tribunals have developed little expertise in the sex discrimination and equal pay legislation and in the issues involved;

(2) that the tribunals do not understand what analysis is expected in sex discrimination and equal pay claims, accepting explanations as they would in claims of unfair dismissal;

(3) that in many cases too little relevant and convincing evidence is being produced to persuade tribunals that discrimination has occurred.

Lack of Tribunal Expertise

It seemed possible that the chairmen and panel members who were making errors simply lacked expertise in the equality legislation. It turned out that they lacked both experience and training and that even the few administrative practices and policies which might assure a more expert panel were widely unknown or ignored.

Expertise of Particular Members of Tribunal

The Chairmen at the Hearings

The industrial tribunal system employs both full-time and part-time chairmen, full-time chairmen being generally regarded as the more experienced. In Scotland, it is the practice *always* to assign sex discrimination and equal pay cases to full-time chairmen and, in fact, in 1980-1982 every case was so assigned.

In England and Wales, the same practice, though espoused by a few administrators, is neither widely known nor followed assiduously in the regional offices visited during this study. In fact, of the 215 sex discrimination and equal pay cases decided on the merits from 1980-1982, 133 cases (62%) were assigned to full-time chairmen, and 82 cases (38%) to part-time chairmen. The record differs with the type of claim heard: full-time chairmen heard 67% of sex discrimination claims but only 49% of equal pay claims. The pattern is different for the 52 preliminary, interlocutory and compensation hearings:[1] in 1980 nearly every one of these was heard by a full-time chairman, but this rate was reduced by nearly half (to 53%) in both 1981 and 1982. A review of the assignment of chairmen at hearings for all tribunal jurisdictions in 1980-1982 demonstrates that full-time chairmen presided over 53.8% of all session days.[2]

Impact upon Complainant Success. While full-time chairmen made their share of errors in the decisions reviewed, it is none the less true that more complainants were successful with full-time chairmen presiding than with part-time chairmen. (Details are provided in Chapter 5.)

Women as Panel Members

Lay members from both sides of industry are regarded as providing the appropriate 'expertise' in the bulk of industrial tribunals' hearings. However, undoubtedly in recognition of the fact that an appreciation of sex discrimination cases may require a more particular expertise and experience, some tribunal administrators attempt to place a woman on each panel hearing a sex discrimination or equal pay claim. It is also thought that the presence of a woman may make the hearing less formidable for women complainants. In fact, several complainants interviewed for this study spontaneously stated that they felt more relaxed because there was a woman on their panel. The policy of including a woman on every panel is in accordance with the Government's 1975 White Paper on sex discrimination[3] and is also consistent with the principle of representative membership which has long been accepted for a variety of tribunals.[4] However, it is not being followed in England and Wales as closely as its importance should require: during the three years studied, a woman was on the panel of 92% of the sex discrimination claims, but of only 77% of the panels in equal pay claims. Moreover, the trend was towards a less faithful adherence: 1982 had the worst record, with 35% of equal pay cases heard by all-male panels.

Similarly, with the 43 preliminary, interlocutory and compensation hearings,[5] the trend was towards fewer women on the panels. Although the overall rate for the three years was 89%, the rate in 1982 was the lowest, with all-male panels deciding about one case in six.

In Scotland, the policy of having a woman on each panel in sex discrimination and equal pay cases is followed assiduously: with at least one woman on the panel of each such case heard in the years 1980-1982. Scotland had a woman in the position of a full-time chair who heard several of the cases, therefore a few panels included two women.

Impact upon Complainant Success. It is also true that complainants heard by tribunals which included a woman were successful more often than those heard by all-male panels. (Details are provided in the statistical analysis of success in Chapter 5).

Total Panel Composition in 1980-1982

A disappointing picture emerged when data on the type of chair and whether the panel included a woman were combined. Complainants *lacked* either a full-time chair or a woman on the panel, or had neither, at 33% of the hearings in 1980, 40% in 1981, and 45% in 1982.

Women Chairing Tribunal Hearings

In England and Wales women were rarely assigned to chair sex discrimination and equal pay tribunal hearings: of the 215 hearings on case merits during 1980-1982 only 11, or 5%, were chaired by women. In the same period, women chaired only two of the 24 preliminary hearings. These figures may seem low; on the other hand, since England and Wales had only one woman as a full-time chair, almost any choice to assign a woman to chair the tribunal was also a choice to assign a part-time chair. This was not the situation in Scotland, which had a woman in the position of a full-time chair who, during the three-year period, was assigned to seven of the 13 hearings on the merits and on preliminary matters.

Expertise through Experience?

With unfair dismissal and redundancy cases, both chairs and panel members commonly gain extensive experience fairly quickly. Several chairmen interviewed for this study estimated that they heard 150-200 unfair dismissal cases a year; and a recent study of panel members' participation in unfair dismissal hearings, revealed that 17% of the 199 members who provided information had sat on more than 26 cases during the preceeding year.[6] This is *not* the case with sex discrimination and equal pay cases. Under the present assignment system, which is wholly random[7], the few cases heard are scattered among a very large number of chairmen and panel members.

Assignment of Tribunal Chairmen

Over the 1980-1982 period, the 215 sex discrimination and equal pay hearings on the merits were distributed among *116 different individuals* as follows:

   (a)   56 chairmen heard 1 case each;
   (b)   33 chairmen heard 2 cases each;
   (c)   20 chairmen heard 3 cases each;
   (d)   5 chairmen heard 4 cases each;
   (e)   1 chairman heard 6 cases; and
   (f)   1 chairman heard 7 cases.[8]

Thus, *only seven chairmen heard more than one case a year,* hardly a number calculated to develop or maintain expertise. It is true that in the early years of the legislation there were large numbers of equal pay cases, so it is possible some chairmen became familiar with equal pay issues at that time. On the other hand, there is no way of knowing whether they are being handled by such chairmen, if they exist, since cases are assigned at random. Forty-five different chairmen handled the 64 additional dispositions reviewed (preliminary, interlocutory, and compensation hearings; applications for review; dismissals for want of prosecution; and settlements and stipulations agreed *after* a hearing had commenced). Moreover, for 10 of these 45 chairmen, the preliminary hearing or application for review was the only sex discrimination or equal pay decision during the three-year period.

Assignment of Panel Members

The situation was even more extreme with panel members, virtually none of whom were assigned to enough sex discrimination and equal pay cases to develop any sort of familiarity with them. Out of a total of 246 sex discrimination and equal pay hearings in 1980-1982, requiring 492 panel 'slots', 379 individuals were assigned *to one case each*; 49 people sat on two cases each and, of these, 29 heard cases which were at least a year apart. Only five individuals sat on three cases, none sitting more frequently.[9] Unlike the situation with unfair dismissal cases, these circumstances appear to make it virtually impossible to expect a panel member or most chairmen to develop any meaningful expertise in sex discrimination or equal pay cases through experience.

Training Tribunal Panels

Particularly in view of the fact that the equality legislation is complex, this lack of experience with the sex discrimination and equal pay legislation might be offset by providing training for chairmen and panel members. However, almost no training is provided to either group.

Chairmen.   Most chairmen interviewed stated that their 'training' involved observing another chairman's hearings for a day. They had received no specific formal training of any kind about the sex discrimination or equal pay legislation. Several stated they would welcome guidance in addressing and resolving the issues such cases raise, including issues of 'justifiability' in indirect discrimination cases, 'red-circling' in equal pay cases, and on the question of drawing inferences from circumstantial evidence.

Panel Members.   The lack of training for panel members in England and Wales has received sustained criticism.[10] At the time of this study, members, who generally have no experience of sex discrimination issues, were being given two half-day training sessions each year. A few regions did more. These sessions sometimes dealt with the equality legislation. Academic commentators, practitioners, and higher court judges alike have noted that the sex discrimination and equal pay legislation is complex. The types of issues and questions raised are very difficult for any lay person to manage without training. Several tribunal chairmen interviewed were concerned about the performance of the panel members in sex discrimination and equal pay cases. These chairmen were, without exception, dedicated to the idea of participation by lay members and were highly respectful of the members' contributions in the bulk of cases. They stated, however, that *both male and female* members are currently *not* qualified to judge equality cases and that either specific experience or special training, or both, is needed to develop their competence to handle the issues these cases present.

One of the more serious opinions expressed was that many lay members (possibly influenced by the previous existence of penal sanctions in racial discrimination cases) attach such a stigma to a finding of discrimination, that they are extremely reluctant to find discrimination has occurred. One chairman interviewed said 'effectively, they apply a standard of proof not simply of "the balance of probabilities" but "not unless absolutely certain"'. It could well be that lay members who feel uninformed on sex discrimination and equal pay issues are particularly reluctant to take active and independent roles at hearings and in decision-making. This would be one explanation for the fact that in the 215 cases reviewed for the period 1980-1982, there were only *two* cases in which a panel member disagreed with the chairman on the disposition of a case, a disagreement rate of less than 1% – lower than the 4% 'dissent' rate in industrial tribunal decisions generally.[11]

Problems with Tribunal Panels

Practitioners, academics and advocacy groups in Britain have identified other ways in which chairmen and panel members are not ideally suited to deciding equality cases, among them their age, sex, and socio-economic backgrounds. Some argue that the panel members' expertise, which is appropriate to unfair dismissal cases, is insufficient or even inappropriate for adjudicating sex discrimination and equal pay cases. They argue that lay members' expertise does *not* extend to questions of discrimination and that their economic and/or social backgrounds are unlikely to have sensitised them to such issues. Laurence Lustgarten has written:

> . . . Precisely because of their membership, the use of industrial tribunals (as the forum to decide employment discrimination cases) may well have been a mistake. Nothing in the background of experiences of most wingmen can be expected to equip them with an understanding of discrimination or empathy with its victims. Indeed, in so far as discrimination has come about through understandings between union and management, or merely as the inadvertent result of long-standing practice, they can be expected to be instinctively unsympathetic to complainants . . .[12]

He identified that what was needed were panel members:

> . . . familiar with the pattern and practices of discrimination, as well as of industrial relations generally, to have a 'feel' for which of the conflicting narrations and explanations of the parties seems more credible.[13]

Others have argued that the tri-partite nature of the tribunal panel is inappropriate:

> . . . Even if the training of tribunal members were improved, the structural composition of the tribunal system gives cause for concern. It is a fact that a policy of sex equality does in various ways disrupt the *status quo*. It is also a fact that both employers and trades unions have expressed resistance to the SDA . . . a tri-partite formula may well be useful in areas where employer and employee associations have different interests and a balance needs to be achieved, but may be less viable in an area such as sex discrimination where the interests of both sides of industry are as likely to coincide as they are to conflict.[14]

In 1973 the NCCL argued that the men involved in the industrial tribunals might themselves be prejudiced against women; they advocated special discrimination tribunals with two women panel members.[15] Others believe that an understanding or appreciation of allegations of sex discrimination is made less likely by the great preponderance of older individuals who serve as panel members: one survey of tribunal members found that two-thirds of the 'employee'-representative members were over 56, with only 6% under 45; and 73% of the 108 'employer' – representative members were over 56 years old, with only 10% below 45.[16] In fact, the industrial tribunals generally have been criticised as having too few younger chairmen and too few women since the early 1970s.[17]

Confusion with Unfair Dismissal?

Sex discrimination and equal pay claims are only a tiny proportion of the cases heard in the industrial tribunals each year. In 1980-1982, there were 215 hearings on sex discrimination and equal pay claims out of a total of 34,982 tribunal hearings.[18] The work of tribunals overwhelmingly consists of hearings on claims of unfair dismissal and unfair selection for redundancy. A number of observations suggest the tribunals may be failing to distinguish appropriately between dismissal/redundancy claims and equal rights claims, particularly those of sex discrimination.

The Legal Standard

In cases of unfair dismissal and unfair selection for redundancy, the employers' decisions and actions are judged upon their 'reasonableness'. This, of course, is not the issue in deciding a sex discrimination claim. The question there is not whether the employer's actions can be considered 'reasonable' or 'fair'. The issue is 'equal treatment' – whether what has been done to the complainant has been or would be done equally to individuals of the other sex who were in a similar situation. A woman's wage may not be a bad wage, but if it is less than that of a man who does the same work it is none the less illegal under the EQPA 1970.

From the cases reviewed, it appears likely that many tribunals, accustomed as they are to unfair dismissal cases and inexperienced as they are in sex discrimination cases, simply ignore the distinction between the two and decide them in the same way. As illustrated in Chapter 2, there were several cases where the tribunal specifically stated the wrong standard. In another 58 decisions out of 129 in total, the tribunal did not state the facts by which it could judge comparative treatment. While it is possible in these cases that those facts were submitted in evidence and considered by the tribunal and simply not mentioned in the decision, this seems unlikely if the tribunal understood that 'equal treatment' was the central issue of the case. In those cases that combined sex discrimination and unfair dismissal claims it was not uncommon to read decisions which stated the 'reasonableness' standard on the unfair dismissal claim, and no different standard for the claim of sex discrimination. A number certainly gave no indication that any different analysis was made in deciding the sex discrimination claim.

Degree of Scrutiny

A further difference between the two types of cases is the degree to which the tribunal must scrutinise the employers' explanation of their actions. The EAT has stated that tribunals must receive from employers in discrimination cases an explanation that is 'clear and specific'.[19] This is more stringent than the attitude tribunals take in unfair dismissal/redundancy cases, where according to knowledgeable commentators, the tribunals are extremely deferential to management prerogative. One commentator, for example, believes an instinctive judicial unwillingness to 'meddle' in managerial decisions has led courts to adopt a 'neutral' approach when interpreting the unfair dismissal legislation, which they view as neutral, but which, in practice, prevents a careful scrutiny of managerial discretion. In support of this contention he cites the often-used standard that tribunals will intervene only 'where no reasonable management could have reached such a decision because it was outside the range of reasonable responses which management could have made'.[20]

Another observes:

> Despite the 'expert' nature of tribunals with their representatives from each side of industry, they are not allowed (by decisions reached in higher courts) to judge an employer's action in dismissing by their *own* view of what would have been reasonable in the circumstances . . . The standard by which they must judge the employer's action is that of the 'reasonable employer' . . . The standards of fairness operated by the tribunals . . . are not those of what might be termed common sense, nor indeed are they those of employees. But they are not even those of the tribunal itself; the tribunals operate *managerial* standards of fairness.[21]

Many decisions reviewed in this study reflect this attitude, particularly in cases where the complainant had combined a claim of sex discrimination with a claim of unfair dismissal/selection for redundancy. The following is a representative description of how the tribunals perceived their task in these cases:

> We are mindful of the fact that we must resist the temptation to substitute our own criteria for selection. We are unanimous that management was justified to select by its criteria as set out in this judgement. We are not called upon to pass any judgement upon it other than on its fairness and we are satisfied that it was as fair a criteria as any other in such catastrophic circumstances and was far from being a criteria that no reasonable employer would apply. *(Delia O'Brien v Schreiber Furniture Ltd)*

This approach is not designed to elicit the 'clear and specific explanation' required from an employer in a sex discrimination case. It can certainly be imagined that where this position is routinely adopted, it may well carry over into the attitudes taken in sex discrimination cases. The possibility that this attitude may affect the tribunals' approach in sex discrimination cases has been noted by an authority on employment law who also serves as a tribunal chairman: Hepple has observed:

> . . . The enormous interplay between the unfair dismissal and discrimination jurisdictions makes the tribunals inclined to respect a wide band of 'reasonable' managerial decisions.[22]

In fact, as discussed in Chapter 2, decisions in many sex discrimination cases were notable for their acceptance of employers' explanations which were vague or involved apparent inconsistencies, and were unsupported by objective or documentary evidence.

Success Rates

A comparison of success rates at hearings yields interesting information. Complainants who claimed unfair dismissal had about the same rate of success on that claim whether or not they also claimed sex discrimination of some sort.[23] However, success with sex discrimination claims when joined with unfair dismissal/ selection for redundancy claims was considerably lower than the success in 'pure' discrimination claims. Sex discrimination claims joined with unfair dismissal or redundancy claims were in 1980 and 1982 extraordinarily less successful than other sex discrimination claims; and over the entire three-year period, the 'joined' claims succeeded only *half* as often as other sex discrimination claims.[24]

It is of course possible that these matters reflect entirely appropriate decisions. For example, sex discrimination claims joined with unfair dismissal claims may have been 'make-weight'. Without a careful analysis of the claims, using the case files and even interviews, it would be impossible to judge whether the decisions were appropriate, especially since so many of the written decisions dismiss the sex discrimination claim without even stating what evidence was presented in support of it. Yet on the basis of the matters mentioned, it appears possible that the figures reflect a lack of attention to those sex discrimination claims which are combined with claims of unfair dismissal, or even error in applying the correct legal standard and type of analysis.

The Scale of the Problem

If tribunals are confusing their analysis of sex discrimination claims with their analysis of claims of unfair dismissal, the problem is substantial, even if the confusion is primarily in those cases which *actually include* both types of claims. For in 1982, 40% of all claims of sex discrimination heard by the tribunals were combined with a claim of unfair dismissal/selection for redundancy, an increase over the percentage in 1980 (31%) and 1981 (32%).[25] Over the three-year period, 16 of the 54 'joined' discrimination claims were claims concerning promotion, recruitment, victimisation, and other areas; 39 were claims of discrimination in *dismissal*, of which 31 concerned dismissal on the grounds of redundancy. Combined claims concerning dismissal were always the largest group, more than doubling in number between 1980 and 1982.

The problem does not appear to be so acute with equal pay claims. From 1980-1982, the tribunals decided 11 cases where equal pay claims were joined with claims of unfair dismissal or unfair selection for redundancy; a total of 19% of all equal pay cases decided. These cases showed no evidence of the confused standards found in cases of sex discrimination in dismissal: a tribunal could simultaneously decide the dismissal had been fair because the complainant had exhibited gross misconduct, and still find her work to have been the same as a male co-worker and award her equal pay *(Mrs Beryl McDade v Bradshaws Motor House Ltd)*. However, even if the tribunals are applying the correct legal standard in equal pay cases, a tendency to accept an employer's statements with less scrutiny than is required might well affect a tribunal's overall analysis, as it does in sex discrimination cases.

Summary

The decisions during 1980-1982 suggest that in many instances tribunals are not appropriately distinguishing the legal standard and type of analysis applicable to sex discrimination cases from that appropriate to claims of unfair dismissal and unfair selection for redundancy. The EAT has recognised this problem in two cases since this study was completed, ordering new hearings on two sex discrimination cases where the tribunals failed to distinguish principles and evidence applicable and relevant in unfair dismissal cases but inappropriate in discrimination claims.[26]

Nature of Evidence

It also seems possible that the tribunals in some cases resorted to judgements on credibility or accepted 'superficial' explanations from respondents, because so little reliable and convincing evidence was submitted by the complainant. A review of the 215 decisions on case merits revealed that a substantial number of cases were decided primarily upon testimonial evidence or upon insignificant documentary evidence.[27]

The following table identifies the types of evidence submitted at hearings.

Table 3.1 *Types of evidence presented at SDA and EQPA hearings, 1980-1982*

		Total
Testimony only	58	(27%)
Testimony and existing documents only	105	(49%)
Testimony, existing documents and prepared documents	24	(11%)
Testimony, documents, s.74 questionnaire, or 'further and better particulars'	21	(10%)
Testimony, documents and expert testimony or site visit	5	(2%)
Agreed facts	2	(1%)
	215	(100%)

Thus, in over one-quarter of the cases, *no* documentary evidence was alluded to at all. Less than one-quarter of the decisions mentioned information especially prepared for the hearing, or specifically directed to the issues involved, e.g., prepared charts, lists and analyses, a s.74 questionnaire or motion for further and better particulars, expert testimony or a site visit. In about half of the cases, the parties presented testimony and a variety of existing documents. When this category was further broken down into 'cases with only one or two documents' (e.g. just the letter of dismissal; just the job application; just the job advertisement), and 'cases with several documents', it appeared that two-thirds of these cases (70) had the lesser number of documents. So, in fully 128 cases – well over half of the total heard – the evidence before the tribunal was only testimony, or testimony and one or two documents.

The amount of evidence available did appear to make a difference in case outcome; over the three-year period, albeit with annual fluctuation within categories, the success rate of complainants rose directly with the amount of documentation available to the tribunal. Table 3.2 provides the figures for the three-year period examined.

Table 3.2   *Types of evidence presented and complainant success at SDA and EQPA hearings, 1980-1982*

	Rate of success %
Testimony only	22
Testimony and existing documents (few)	27
Testimony and existing documents (several)	28
Testimony and documents prepared for the hearing	42
Testimony and s.74 'further and better particulars', experts, and/or site visits	46
Agreed facts	50

This difference became more pronounced each year until, in 1982, in hearings where only testimony and existing documents were presented, complainants won 24% of the cases, while in cases where the 'specialised' evidence was presented, they won 70% of the cases. This evidence certainly cannot be considered conclusive because of the subjective nature of the classifications and the uncertainty involved in using decisions in this way. However, it seems reasonable to give credence to what these figures suggest: that the success rate is much higher when there is specialised evidence than where there is only testimony.

Further support for the idea that the tribunals' acceptance of general explanations from respondents is due to lack of sufficient evidence from complainants is found in the quite remarkable difference in success rates among complainants who presented witnesses and those who did not. Table 3.3 provides the figures for the three-year period examined.

Table 3.3   *Witnesses presented and complainant success at SDA and EQPA hearings, 1980-1982*

	Complainant only %	One witness %	Two witnesses %
SDA Claims	17 won	50 won	78 won
EQPA Claims	29 won	33 won	33 won

It is of course common sense to expect that credible corroborative evidence should tend to increase a party's chance of success. However, this difference seems so stark as to suggest that information from a complainant alone often proves insufficient to convince a tribunal.

Inappropriate, Insufficient, Irrelevant Evidence

Tribunals often found the evidence which was presented unhelpful or insufficient. In fact the decisions reveal an overwhelmingly frequent failure by complainants and their representatives to identify correctly in advance the information which was necessary to support the claim, to obtain it, and to produce it in the necessary form at the tribunal hearing. The case decisions are full of references to these failures: the failure to bring necessary witnesses, the presentation of unhelpful witnesses, the failure to present relevant statistics, the failure to bring comparative evidence, the failure to bring sufficiently extensive information to prove a 'pattern' of behaviour, etc. Among the 215 decisions from 1980-1982, there were 50 in which either the tribunal itself specifically described some failure of the complainant or her representative, or in which one could see readily that insufficient information had been offered on the complainant's behalf. Three recurring problems are discussed below: the failure to bring necessary witnesses and to question opposing witnesses effectively; the failure to present basic or comparative evidence; and the failure to produce sufficient statistical evidence.

Absence of Crucial Witnesses and Ineffective Cross-Examination

Tribunals dismissed 10 cases noting specifically that a complainant had brought no corroborating witnesses or had brought witnesses whose testimony was unhelpful. In another seven cases, the tribunals mentioned the complainant's failure to obtain information from the respondent's witness(es), usually their failure to cross-examine, or their failure to do so effectively. For example, in one case where a complainant appeared by herself, the tribunal said:

> The applicant also said that she had acted as a project manager on one occasion whereas Mrs Dent had not. Neither of these matters was put to the respondents' witnesses in cross-examination, and accordingly we had no evidence from the respondents' witnesses in regard thereto. *(Miss Bowman v Data Logic Ltd (A C Cossor Ltd)*

In another case where two women who had lost their part-time jobs claimed unfair dismissal, unfair selection for redundancy and indirect discrimination, the tribunal stated:

> The applicants have conducted their own case. (The respondent's solicitor) has called the respondent's Operations Manager . . . in order that the two applicants should be enabled to cross-examine him, which indeed they have done, although in the particular circumstances ineffectually. *(Mrs Kidd and Mrs Maggs v DRG (UK) Ltd)*

In all of these cases, where information about representation was provided in the decision, the complainant was unrepresented or had a representative who was not legally qualified.

Use of Written Statements

Parties (particularly complainants) frequently submitted written statements to the tribunal to substitute for the testimony of a witness, where the individual in question was unable for some reason to attend the tribunal hearing. There were several cases in which complainants had brought what they considered to be a viable substitute for live testimony, but were informed by the tribunal that the statement was virtually worthless. Some tribunals appeared to take the position that the trouble lay not with written statements generally but with those which were not *sworn*. An example was a case where a male complainant claimed sex discrimination in the respondents' refusal to hire him as a care assistant. He had found another job as a care assistant by the date of his hearing, but submitted two written statements through his representative. The tribunal said:

Neither of those were sworn, and in the absence of any sworn evidence by the applicant, and any opportunity for his evidence to be tested by cross-examination, his statements cannot carry the same measure of credibility as they would had they constituted sworn evidence. *(Mr Stubbs v B and R J Hughesdon)*

The matron of the respondent nursing home testified she 'had no recollection of speaking to the complainant, or indeed any male applicant, for the position advertised'. This evidence was contradicted by the matron's own evidence on other points yet, on this basis, the tribunal dismissed the case.

It is worth noting that a number of the parties interviewed for this study were surprised by the tribunals' sceptical attitude towards written statements, even where they were brought for 'good' reasons (the individual must attend school, has a new job, etc.). Of course, the underlying reason for this attitude is the valid concern that on important questions, persons should be available to be seen, heard and questioned by the tribunal. Nonetheless, this position does surprise a number of people who attend hearings, some of whom lose their cases due to their ignorance of this tribunal attitude.

Lack of Comparative Evidence

A few tribunal decisions stated that the complainants had brought no evidence in support of their sex discrimination claims and dismissed them *(Mrs Robinson v Tees Components Ltd; Mrs M A Robins v UBM)*. A number of complainants apparently did not bring the very basic information required to establish their claim, such as one male complainant who claimed discrimination in recruitment for a job. Unrepresented, he brought sufficient information to establish that discrimination had occurred, but provided no information (even his own testimony) about any other job applicants. The tribunal said:

> There was no evidence which would have enabled the tribunal to decide whether or not the applicant would have been appointed to the job had he not been discriminated against, and as a result, the tribunal is not able to find that the applicant suffered any financial loss as a result of being discriminated against. *(Mr Court v EMI Film and Theatre Corp Ltd)*

The tribunal merely awarded the complainant £50 for injury to feelings.

Some complainants presented their cases lacking basic information obtainable using a s.74 questionnaire. In one obvious case a tribunal noted:

> No questionnaire under section 74 of the Sex Discrimination Act 1975 has been issued on the applicant's behalf. Had it been, the crucial issue as to who took the decision to take the applicant off the test rig could have been clarified before the hearing. As it was, the applicant admitted in cross-examination 'I was not aware it was Mr Watson's decision to take me off testing'. It was therefore not until that point that it became known that the respondent's case was that the decision was taken by Mr Watson. *(Mrs Humphries v Dunlop Ltd)*

In several other cases where some evidence on the respondent's workforce – or at least comparative evidence of some sort – would have been necessary to win the case, the complainant or their representative apparently did not present it. In a few cases, the tribunals noted the lack of comparative evidence. In others, the tribunals simply accepted a respondent's anecdotal, limited evidence of equal treatment of women, since the complainant offered no detailed evidence to discredit or rebut it.

Insufficient Statistical Evidence

Statistical evidence can be a crucial factor in establishing the likelihood that discrimination has occurred. Indeed as Lustgarten has discussed, it is important in proving both direct and indirect discrimination: in cases of direct discrimination, to 'undermine' or buttress the credibility of witnesses, and with allegations of indirect discrimination, as direct evidence of existing disparities.[28] Yet there were notable instances where complainants and/or their representatives failed to present relevant or convincing statistical evidence, a matter on which a few tribunals commented specifically. For example, during a hearing on a woman's claim of sex discrimination in promotion, her union officer introduced evidence to prove there was sex discrimination in promotions throughout her department. The tribunal said:

> . . . when a tabulated list of these appointments (A26) was produced, (the union District Officer) cross-examined in detail to show that, prior to the restructuring promotions, there had only been four women involved, one of whom had a promotion in name only, another was an initial appointment, the third involved the transition from trainee/programmer to programmer, and Mrs Murray's was the only clear

promotion. (The union officer) made the general point that, in what must be presumed to be a large department, these instances must point toward very limited female promotions and must support the applicant's case. We consider that if there had been any substance in this point detailed evidence would have been put before us. The applicant was represented by a [union] official. If it had been desired to put this issue in concrete form, a statistical exercise could have been carried out by which the number of promotions was contrasted with the number of persons in the department and this shown over a number of years. As is obvious from the course of other sex discrimination cases, this can be vital evidence. *(Mrs Bell v Newcastle-upon-Tyne City Council)*

Grading Systems Cases

The lack of necessary evidence was apparent in three equal pay claims involving grading systems *(Mrs Lewis v SGS Inspection Services Ltd; Mrs Harper v Lonsdale Technical Ltd; Mrs Stanger v Efford Experimental Horticultural Station)*. Each case involved the claim that, although a grading system existed, it was not 'fairly applied irrespective of sex' and, in each, this allegation seemed – on the facts related – to be eminently possible. However, in no case did the complainant's representative, at least two of whom were not legally qualified, present enough evidence for the tribunal to so find: the representative offered only one or two examples of other employees who were accorded 'different' treatment.

This is an area in which the tribunals appear particularly reluctant to find that sex discrimination has occurred. They interpret *National Vulcan Engineering Insurance Group Ltd v Wade*[29] – perhaps overly restrictively – as setting an extremely difficult task for a complainant who alleges that a grading system was applied in a discriminatory manner. Yet in these three cases, the evidence which was presented by the complainant could almost be described as anecdotal; certainly a far more complete picture of the effect of the grading system would have been necessary to convince most tribunals. There was no indication that any of the representatives handling these cases had attempted to use advance discovery or the s.74 questionnaire to obtain such information.

Evidence of Indirect Discrimination

Tribunal decisions also noted the lack of necessary information on various aspects of indirect discrimination cases. In one such case, the tribunal commented in detail on the presentation by the complainant's union representative:

It was submitted for Mrs Wright that the earlier discrimination against women by way of the 28 years age limit for outside entrants for the post of Executive Officer (as decided by the *Price* case) as it related to the 24% of Executive Officers recruited by direct entry, was reflected in the disproportionate numbers of male Executive Officers in the Civil Service and that this resulted in discrimination against Mrs Wright.

We could only assume that had (the union representative) pursued the argument further, it would be, that since women were discriminated against in the direct entry to the Executive Officer grade in the Civil Service by the age limit of 28, the result was that there were more men than women in the 24% who actually entered, and had there not been this earlier discrimination, more women would have formed part of the 24% (presumably at a later age than 28) and there would thus be more women unable to comply with the age limit . . .

There was no quantification of any kind put forward on behalf of the applicant of what those effects might have been in relation to the 24% of direct entry Executive Officers, thus making more women eligible for the Administration Trainee Competition with the result that more of these would be barred by the age limit of under 32 giving a considerably smaller proportion who would be eligible, and fulfilling the requirement in section 1(1) (b) of the Act . . .

We did not think that the submission put forward on behalf of the applicant succeeded. *(Mrs Wright v Civil Service Commission)*

Whose Responsibility: The Tribunals' or the Parties'?

This study identifies two types of problems. One is those due largely to a lack of expertise in the sex discrimination and equal pay legislation; these include actual errors in applying statutory provisions, using an incorrect legal standard, and giving weight to matters which are clearly irrelevant to claims of sex discrimination. Also included in this group are problems associated with the inconsistencies in tribunals' decisions which have arisen primarily where some tribunals have used an outdated or erroneous approach to certain issues. The second group of problems relates to complainants' insufficient fact development and case presentations – in some instances the problem of simply submitting too little evidence to support a claim and, in others, submitting evidence which is inappropriate or even irrelevant to the discrimination alleged. Where does responsibility for these problems lie: with the tribunals or with the parties? In theory the lines of responsibility should be apparent; in reality the situation is not so clear.

Expertise in the Legislation

For the most part, one would consider expertise in the legislation to be the responsibility of the tribunal: it is the official forum to which lay persons submit their claims, and it is their role to decide these claims in light of the applicable legislation. At least one should be able to expect from the tribunal a knowledge of major statutory provisions, of the correct legal standard, and of relevant decisions reached by the higher courts. On the other hand, it is unquestionable that a tribunal can be substantially aided by a knowledgeable presentation by the parties. Several of the tribunal chairmen most experienced with sex discrimination and equal pay cases stated that knowledgeable legal representation is extremely helpful, if not necessary, in such cases. They look to informed solicitors or counsel to develop and present the facts, to relate the facts to the applicable legislative provisions, to provide productive and relevant examination of the witnesses, to argue points of law, and to suggest the inferences which they believe should be drawn from circumstantial evidence. Indeed the case decisions document several instances where tribunals felt limited by the lack of 'quality' legal representation. In an equal pay case where the employer conceded 'like work' but claimed the case involved 'red circling', the tribunal commented:

> This is not a simple case and we feel bound to say that we would have hoped for a more helpful presentation of it on the part of the respondents, on whom the burden of proof lies [on the issue of red-circling]. No authorities were cited to us by (the respondent's solicitor), although there is now a fairly large body of relevant case law. *(Mr Emery v Somerset Police Authority)*

Another chairman, a recognised expert in the area, heard two cases where full adjudication was restricted because, although the complainant had legal representation, the respondent did not. In the first, his decision stated:

> *Was there indirect discrimination under section 1(1)(b) or section 3(1)(b)?* In view of our finding on the direct discri-

mination point, it is not necessary for us to consider this question. Mr Shirley was not represented and did not appear to appreciate the full implications of the indirect discrimination provisions, although the Tribunal attempted to explain them to him, and we did not have the benefit of full argument, and we prefer not to express any view on this aspect of the case. *(Mrs Shirley Ali Khan v Kent Country Nurseries Ltd)* (emphasis in the original)

In the second, where the complainant claimed equal pay with her male successor, her solicitor referred to the decisions of the Court of Appeal and the European Court of Justice in *Macarthys Ltd v Smith*[30] The chairman wrote:

The respondents were not legally represented and accordingly the Tribunal did not have the benefit of adequate legal argument on the very complex issues which arise as to the application of these decisions to the facts of the present case and as to the interaction of the 1970 Act and Article 119 of the Treaty of Rome. *(Miss Stankovich v Phillips Mans Shops Ltd)*

The importance of knowledgeable representation was also evident in that the quality of the analysis presented by several Chairmen was distinctly superior in those cases where the complainant had been well represented.

Fact Development and Case Presentation

In an adversarial system such as the tribunals, obtaining and presenting the evidence to establish a claim are regarded as the task of the parties. This is surely unrealistic in sex discrimination and equal pay cases, however, given that half of all complainants are unrepresented and that the law is generally regarded as quite complex. Nearly all the cases reviewed in which tribunals commented upon problems with evidence and presentation concerned those where complainants were unrepresented or where they had lay representatives. In fact, recognising these difficulties, some tribunal panels do attempt actively to assist the parties. The importance of this matter underlined the need to determine how in practice this responsibility was being borne, or shared, by parties and the tribunals. Attention was given to whether representation makes a difference in case presentation and the quality of analysis and, if so, whether some types of representation are more effective than others. Further, since complainants with representation are still the exception, the question as to whether tribunals generally attempt to assist the parties and, where they do, the degree to which they are successful, was examined in some detail.

Representation

It is evident from comments in the tribunal decisions reviewed that a lack of knowledge, both about basic tribunal procedure and about the sex discrimination and equal pay legislation, has frequently resulted in tribunal presentations which are seriously lacking in appropriate and necessary evidence. It is also evident that this is occurring even in many of those cases where the complainant is represented. For example, tribunals criticised the failure to present crucial witnesses or to cross-examine effectively both where complainants were unrepresented and where they had non-legal representation; in almost all of the cases in which written statements were presented instead of live witnesses the complainants were represented by trade union officials and other lay representatives. And in five of the six cases in which tribunals stated that the statistical evidence presented was insufficient, the complainants were represented: four by their trade union representatives and one by her father. This situation is distinctly different from that, for example, in National Insurance tribunals and in Supplementary Benefit Appeal tribunals, where studies found that success rates for those who were represented were dramatically higher than for those who were unrepresented – *irrespective of the type of representation.*[31] In handling sex discrimination and equal pay cases, it seems that the *type* of representation can make a very substantial difference.[32] Precisely which type of representation will provide a difference is somewhat less clear.

Legal Representation

There is some evidence that lawyers provided the most effective representation, particularly when in opposition to non-legally trained individuals. In England and Wales, where representation was unequal, the legally qualified representatives did distinctly better than other individuals. As Table 3.4 shows, in a sample of 58 hearings from 1980-1982 at which representation of both parties could be determined and where respondents had legal representation, complainants' success rates decreased dramatically with the decrease in expertise of their representatives.

Table 3.4 *Parties' relative types of representation and complainant success at SDA and EQPA hearings, 1980-1982*

Number of Cases	Complainant Representation	Respondent Representation	Complainant Success Rate %
24	Legal	Legal	46
13	Trade union	Legal	38
13	Self	Legal	23
4	Husband, father, friend	Legal	0
4	CAB, Law Centre, etc.	Legal	0

This situation of unequal representation is likely to be frequent: complainants were self-represented or had lay representatives at about 50% of all hearings; whereas respondents were represented by lawyers, managers, or employers' associations at more than 90% of all hearings.

Knowledgeable Representation

However, several chairmen stated that legal qualification itself does not assure good representation on sex discrimination or equal pay claims: certainly the case decisions contain several examples of incorrect advice, poor fact development, and errors in presentation by solicitors, as well as by non-legally qualified individuals. Their opinion is that it is representation by solicitors and barristers who are familiar with the relevant legislation which is essential. One said that representation by solicitors who did not know the legislation was 'useless', another that it 'hindered development of the facts'. It seems that the more accurate conclusion is that the best representation is by individuals who are knowledgeable about the particular provisions of the sex discrimination and equal pay legislation, and skilled in developing and presenting cases under this legislation. This would appear to be true of trade union representatives and lawyers alike: those who are knowledgeable do skilful jobs in these cases; those who simply rely on their knowledge of other employment legislation, quite often do not.

Effect of Representation on Outcome of Case

Data on the success rate of complainants with different types of representation tend to support this conclusion. EOC-assisted representatives (who were primarily skilled lawyers advised by the EOC's own legal section) were far more successful than lawyers as a whole. In 1980-1982 EOC-assisted representatives won 41% of all the cases they handled at hearings, while, as a group, other lawyers won 24% and 28% of their sex discrimination and equal pay hearings respectively. The magnitude of this difference, however, may be due in part to the fact that the EOC is somewhat selective in the cases it chooses to support.

This was also the case in Northern Ireland, where the EOC of Northern Ireland (a separate entity from the EOC of England, Scotland and Wales) provides representation in a high percentage of cases heard: since 1980 there has been EOC-assisted representation for 85% of all complainants, of whom 55% were successful at hearings: 71% of those with equal pay hearings and 46% of those with sex discrimination hearings.[33]

On the other hand, DE statistics for 1976-1983[34] suggest that the type of representation may be less important in determining outcome in equal pay cases. For, while in sex discrimination cases legally qualified representatives had by far the highest success rate, at hearings on equal pay claims the success rates of the various types of representatives were quite similar. This could be due to the fact that issues normally raised in equal pay cases – rates of pay, similarities and differences in work, etc, and the type of evidence required – may be more familiar to lay persons from their own work experience particularly trade union shop stewards and other officers.

Complainants themselves seem to recognise that expert knowledge is necessary in sex discrimination and equal pay cases. Despite the fact that the numbers of applications to tribunals decreased from 1980-1982, requests for legal assistance from the EOC actually increased. Each year the EOC was able to grant only half of the requests it received.[35] Indeed, it is still true that in equal rights cases a complainant with skilled representation remains the exception rather than the rule. The question that naturally arises is whether, in ordinary circumstances, the tribunals can fill this gap.

The Tribunals' Role

In a number of the decisions quoted in this chapter, tribunals faulted unrepresented complainants for not eliciting crucial information from respondents' witnesses. It seems reasonable to ask why, in such a situation, the tribunal itself did not do so. Where a complainant's representative did not know to offer information about how employees of the other sex were treated – or promoted, or selected for redundancy – why didn't the tribunal *ask* for the information? An accurate answer would be that in such situations, some tribunals *would* ask the questions while others would not. A surprising range of attitudes exist among chairmen and panel members on their role at hearings, both about whether they should intervene at all and, among those who believe in intervention, about the circumstances in which, and the extent to which, it is appropriate.

Rules of Procedure

The rules of procedure which regulate the tribunals[36] permit a great deal of tribunal participation and direction of the applications and hearings procedure. For example:

> A tribunal may . . . if it thinks fit of its own motion . . . (i) require a party to furnish in writing . . . further particulars of the grounds on which he or it relies, and on any facts and contentions relevant thereto . . . (Rule 4).

> The tribunal shall conduct the hearing in such a manner as it considers most suitable to the clarification of the issues before it and generally to the just handling of the proceedings . . . (Rule 8).

And a 'hearing' is defined as:

> . . . a sitting of tribunal duly constituted for the purpose of receiving evidence, hearing addresses, and witnesses *or doing anything lawfully requisite* to enable the tribunal to reach a decision on any question . . . (Rule 2). (emphasis added)

Further, a tribunal is not bound by the rules concerning the admissibility of evidence applicable in courts of law. (Rule 8) These rules give tribunals considerable power to direct hearings and case presentation. On the other hand, the tribunals are generally regarded as adversarial, not inquisitorial, in nature. The Industrial Relations Court has actually ruled that the tribunals do *not* have a duty to ensure that all relevant evidence is before it; and that this is the sole responsibility of the parties, whether represented or not.[37]

In view of this somewhat ambiguous situation, a degree of diversity in tribunals' practice is perhaps to be expected. However, both the written decisions and the hearings observed indicate a considerable variation.

Active Tribunals

Among the few examples of an active approach, one case included a quote from a tribunal chairman who stated the general argument for active tribunal inquiry. In this case there had been serious workforce opposition to a woman employee who had applied for a job traditionally reserved for men. The Chairman explained:

We also looked to some extent at the job evaluation exercise which was in progress at the time of Miss Martin's application for the Standby Burner's job. No question as to the validity or fairness of the job evaluation exercise was directly an issue in Miss Martin's application to the tribunal, but in our view it was relevant to investigate whether the job evaluating exercise disclosed any evidence of a discriminatory attitude on the part of management in addition to the discriminatory policy of the union branch. The onus of proving discrimination under United Kingdom law is upon the applicant, and it is usually very difficult to prove. *If the legislation is to be at all effective otherwise than in respect of the most blatant cases (which are very rare) it is necessary that tribunals should themselves probe for evidence of discrimination where a claim is made and there appears to be reasonable suspicion that it may exist.* Evidence of discrimination in one aspect of a particular employment situation would tend to add weight to such evidence as the applicant is able to bring to prove discrimination in respect of the specific matter to which her claim relates. *(Theresa Martin v Tate and Lyle Food and Distribution Ltd)* (emphasis added)

At one hearing, not attended by the complainant, the tribunal raised the question as to whether a certain job requirement might be discriminatory:

We also think it right in this case that we should consider the question of sex discrimination, because certain matters were raised in relation to the physical strength or stamina of the applicant. Under section 6(2) of the Sex Discrimination Act 1975 it is unlawful for a person, in the case of a woman employed by him in an establishment in Great Britain, to discriminate against her by dismissing her, or subjecting her to any other detriment. Under section 7 there can be circumstances where there is a genuine occupational qualification for a job which excuses what might otherwise have been discrimination, but that cannot relate to the physical strength or stamina of women in general. We are satisfied on the evidence in this case, that the selection of the applicant, having regard to the question of physical strength or stamina, was made specifically by looking at the physical strength and stamina of the three individuals and not on the basis of their sex. We conclude that the respondents reasonably came to the conclusion that the two younger men had more physical strength and were more physically capable of carrying out the harder manual work in connection with the hand presses and the handling of materials in the Assembly Department. *(Mrs Roye v C L Equipments Ltd)*

Three other instances of significant tribunal intervention were documented in the decisions. At one preliminary hearing, the tribunal telephoned the absent respondent to learn the size of his workforce *(Mrs Lewis v Havilland Electric Co)*; and in two cases chairmen identified from the case papers possible victimisation claims and notified the parties that the issue might be addressed. *(Mrs Grace-Walsh v Andrew Page Ltd; Mrs Maitland v Edna's Wool Shop)*

Non-Intervention
Yet there were other tribunals which clearly did not assume such a role. One, having identified a probable Sex Discrimination Act violation, clearly believed it was not its task to pursue it. The application had been brought by a male manager of a clothing shop who had been dismissed when the respondents' chain of stores stopped selling men's clothing and began to sell only women's clothes. The tribunal found his dismissal unfair, and said:

> Indeed [the respondents] have been very unforthcoming in stating any reason at all [for the dismissal]. *That is perhaps not surprising when one considers the provisions of the Sex Discrimination Act into which we needn't go, but quite plainly their actions could well be infringing that. (John Calvin Harries v Irvine Sellars Ltd).* (emphasis added)

The tribunal went no further.
A similar attitude was taken by a tribunal in another case. A male manager of a shop which sold men's and women's clothing was replaced with a woman when the shop began to sell only women's clothes. The tribunal stated:

> It is quite clear to this tribunal that this dismissal was unfair: there was no warning and the only reason was that the employer preferred a woman to a man and made no attempt to justify this. *(Mr Fice v Moods Fashions)*

Yet the tribunal did not even allude to the possible violation of the SDA 1975, suggesting either that the tribunal did not consider it was its role to raise the matter or – worse still – did not even realise that the SDA 1975 may have been violated.

Another tribunal appeared to be unwilling to enquire about possible injury to feelings under the SDA 1975. It found that a young woman's dismissal by owners of a chain of clothing shops was *both* unfair and a violation of the SDA 1975. However, in awarding damages, the tribunal, having calculated the 'basic' award and 'compensatory' award for the unfair dismissal, said:

> Because of this order in respect of unfair dismissal, no additional award is being made in respect of the unlawful sex discrimination, which the tribunal has found proved. *(Mrs McKenna v UDS Tailoring Ltd)*

The tribunal did not refer to, or enquire about, the possibility of injured feelings or associated compensation. Alternatively this tribunal may not have been aware that injury to feelings could be compensated under the SDA 1975.

In one case a tribunal found no discrimination had occurred in the selection of the complainant for redundancy, but itself described a situation in which she might well have been entitled to a period of equal pay; however, this issue was not directly addressed *(Mrs Turner v FTL Co Ltd)*. There were also tribunal decisions which recorded testimony about respondents' recruitment or hiring practices, or job assignment procedures, which were very probably discriminatory, but about which the tribunals made no comment *(Mrs Whittier v Alexr Sharp and Co Ltd; Mr Bartlett v St Catherine's Freezer Ctrs Ltd)*. In addition, there were at least four other cases where the facts suggested the possibility that the complainant's dismissal was directly related to her request for equal pay or her act of filing a tribunal application – yet the decisions contained no discussion or findings on those matters, and did not even identify victimisation as a possible issue *(Miss Morton v Sefton Area Health Authority; Mrs Linton, Wigmore, Brewster and Bishop v Bristol Steel Corporation; Mrs Gillman v Dolling Marketing International; Miss Karen Figg v British Tissues Ltd)*. Again, an alternative explanation for the tribunals' lack of comment is that they did not themselves recognise these situations as potentially discriminatory.

Questioning by the chairman and panel members occurred at nearly every hearing observed. However, in only one case (where both parties were represented by solicitors) did the chairman intervene to the extent of pressing reluctant witnesses and challenging others on their testimony. In the others, questions were fewer and largely for clarification or explanation of a particular matter which the panel had not understood; in no case did questioning go beyond matters raised first by the parties. Questions from panel members were fewer than those from chairman and, with a single exception, were all asked merely to clarify earlier testimony. This was quite different from the hearings observed in Scotland, where a far more active approach is taken (see below). In England and Wales, however, tribunals generally appeared reluctant to intervene significantly in the hearing process.

Limited Tribunal Participation

Since some degree of participation by the tribunals is accepted, and even widespread, what can explain their failure to participate more actively in sex discrimination and equal pay cases? It may in part be related to their lack of expertise in sex discrimination and equal pay issues. It certainly appears likely that both chairmen and panel members would intervene more frequently, appropriately and effectively, if they were more familiar with the legislation a case involves. As an extreme example, the tribunal which believes the applicable legal standard to be 'reasonableness' might well not consider it necessary to question a respondent's proffered explanation in much detail.

A different explanation for the general failure to participate actively in hearings is offered by a number of chairmen quite knowledgeable about the applicable law. They feel that active participation sacrifices the tribunal's appearance of objectivity in the eyes of the parties. This risk, they say, dissuades them from questioning as often or forcefully as they might feel useful or even necessary. One chairman interviewed explained, 'we can *obtain* information, but we simply *cannot* cross-examine; it is therefore of quite limited use in cases such a these'. Ironically, this apprehension results in tribunals being least willing to question the parties in the situation where such assistance is probably the most needed: where one or both of the parties is unrepresented. The behaviour of the chairmen at the several hearings observed was consistent with this explanation: they participated much more actively at the hearings where both parties were represented by solicitors than they did where one or both of the parties were unrepresented. With unrepresented parties, they *did* ask questions but they did not pursue answers at any length, even where they were clearly incomplete or contradictory or unresponsive.

It is therefore worth noting that those parties interviewed generally did *not* object to questioning by the tribunal – nor did they take offence at pressing questions: this appeared to be accepted as normal procedure, whether or not they were represented. At two hearings where the parties were unrepresented, the impression was that their objection lay with the abrupt, and in one case, condescending, tenor of the questions, but not to the questioning itself. In fact, a few individuals (particularly those who were unrepresented and had difficulty with presenting witnesses or cross-examining an opponent) wished the chairman had assisted them more. This suggests that tribunals' fears that active questioning might damage their image of impartiality may be exaggereated. A final, and obvious possibility is that many tribunals simply do not see participation in a hearing as their role. In their view, proceedings are adversarial and the task of framing the issues, presenting the evidence, and examining witnesses belongs to the parties.

In contrast, the general attitude among Scottish chairmen is towards more active intervention. Several stated that both in unfair dismissal cases and on sex discrimination and equal pay claims they commonly take quite an active role in eliciting evidence, even to the point of suggesting adjournments so that individuals who would be helpful witnesses could be called. This was certainly the case at a hearing on a claim of sex discrimination in promotion observed in Glasgow. Although the complainants were represented, the chairman and panel members politely but carefully questioned both parties and their witnesses, carrying the examination much further than it had been by the representatives. The Scottish attitude is permitted by Rule 8 of the Scottish tribunals' rule of procedure which, in addition to providing for the avoidance of formality in their proceedings, provides specifically that:

> The tribunal shall conduct the hearing in such a manner as it considers most suitable to the clarification of the issues before it and to the just handling of the proceedings . . . (Rule 8(1)).

One experienced Scottish chairman has commented:

> The Regulations are clearly designed to enable tribunals to carry out their task by allowing them to regulate their own procedure . . . it is important that we take hold of cases at an early stage – by, for example, requiring further particulars of applications and answers, where these are clearly inadequate.
>
> . . . tribunals have a duty to seek out the true issues between the parties and have them focused in the pleadings, if possible. Our practice, and probably the practice of others, is

to scrutinise the Application and Notice of Appearance and to require these documents to be amplified or clarified as necessary. It is, of course, seldom possible to go beyond that – the selection of witnesses and the production of documents is something which the parties must do for themselves, in the first instance. Nevertheless, if we find in the course of a hearing that, for instance, an unrepresented Applicant has failed to ask for documents or to have witnesses cited through ignorance, we would take steps to secure the production or attendance of them before the case was decided. Likewise, if we found it very difficult to decide a case depending on credibility without the evidence of a crucial witness, we would adjourn and have the witness cited to an adjourned hearing. . . . that is what Regulation 8 is for. The only over-riding stipulation is that the Tribunal must act, and be seen to act, in an even-handed manner.[38]

Reasons for Limited Tribunal Participation

On the other hand, in both England and Wales, and Scotland there are certainly very considerable limitations to the contribution chairmen can make by questioning. This is largely due to the fact that chairman and panel members almost always have their first and only contact with the parties at the hearing. Parties may arrive at the hearing without documents to support their positions; they may not have brought a witness the tribunal would wish to hear; or they may present claims of such complexity as to make it impossible effectively to 'develop' the case 'on the spot.' For example, in the many cases where an employer explains his actions in recruiting, promoting, or dismissing an individual on the basis of the person's relative 'potential' or 'performance' – offering no documentation as proof, but only testimonial evidence – the tribunal is left with the choice of simply accepting what is said or, at best, attempting to question them on their opinions, without the benefit of background information. In some cases, employers will have made employment decisions on judgements of character or personality – opinions which are essentially impossible to question without extensive knowledge of the situation and the individuals involved. Claims of indirect discrimination, or of a pattern of discrimination, obviously *cannot* be developed through questioning undertaken for the first time at the hearing by a tribunal chairman or panel. The same would obviously be true of situations in which it became evident *at the hearing* that the alleged discrimination might be by someone *other* than the named respondent, for example, the complainant's trade union. At that stage, tribunal intervention could not rectify the mistake already made.

There is widespread acceptance of the view that the system is fundamentally adversarial and that the role of the tribunal is therefore clearly limited. Hepple has summarised these limitations succinctly:

> The litigation in both the county courts and the tribunals is essentially adversarial. The parties decide when to start and stop the case and what evidence to produce. The courts and tribunals cannot, save on the application of a party, compel the attendance of witnesses or the production of documents or join additional parties who may have an interest. They are restricted to the material presented by the parties which they cannot augment. The chairman and members of an industrial tribunal tend to adopt a far more investigative role than the judge in the county court, but even then there are limits because the tribunal must not give the appearance of favouring one side rather than the other. A recent case had to go all the way to a Court of Appeal before it was confirmed that it was not improper for a tribunal to ask a solicitor, defending a complainant that he had refused to employ a shorthand typist on grounds of her colour, whether the firm had any black employees.[39]

The diversity among chairmen and the distinctly different attitude taken in Scotland suggest there are some alternatives to this situation even under existing rules. However, in general, as the system presently operates, assistance by tribunal panels is not compensating for inadequate or unskilled case preparation or presentation in equal rights cases, and, in most instances, cannot be expected to do so.

Notes

1   These were 25 preliminary hearings, 23 interlocutory hearings and four hearings on compensation. The number is greater than those reported for panel members because it includes some dispositions made by chairmen alone.
2   Information provided by COIT. Full-time chairmen presided over 24,485 of 45,504 session days.
3   See HMSO 1974, para. 83: 'The number of women appointed to the tribunals is being increased. The aim is to have sufficient women so that at least one person of each sex will normally be on a tribunal which is hearing a sex discrimination or equal pay case'.

4 Lustgarten (1980), p197.

5 These were 25 preliminary hearings, 14 interlocutory hearings, and four hearings on compensation.

6 Dickens (1983), p31.

7 Interviews with administrative personnel in the southern and western regions.

8 These figures were arrived at by using the printed tribunal decisions, which always include the chairman's name.

9 These figures are developed from the tribunal decisions, which name the panel members at the hearing. The compilations were done manually, and because of the large number of names involved, there is a slight possibility of minor error.

10 Whitesides and Hawker (1975), p34. Byrne and Lovenduski (1978), p156.

11 Dickens (1983), p30.

12 Lustgarten (1980), p195, discusses the SDA 1975 and the Race Relations Act 1976.

13 Lustgarten (1980).

14 Byrne and Lovenduski (1978), p157.

15 NCCL (1973).

16 Dickens (1983), p29.

17 Whitesides and Hawker (1975), p33.

18 *Department of Employment Gazette*, (December 1981, December 1982, and October 1983). There were 10,037 unfair dismissal hearings in 1980; 13,346 in 1981; and 11,509 in 1982.

19 *Khanna v Ministry of Defence* [1981] 1RLR 331, 333.

20 Collins (1982), and Bowers and Clarke (1981).

21 Dickens and Jones (1981), p11-12. Dickens has subsequently published *Dismissed* (1985). But see Elias (1981).

22 Hepple (1983), p83. He says 'The essential point (in discrimination cases) is that the Court of Appeal expects a process of fact evaluation in an area where no consensus exists among tribunal members, even less a social consensus. The situation is quite different when tribunals determine whether or not an employer has acted reasonably in a case of alleged unfair dismissal. There the tribunals apply the current consensus of what constitutes "good industrial relations practice" (as crystallised in Codes of Practice and EAT Guidelines). Not surprisingly, 96 per cent of decisions are unanimous. The tribunals reflect the norms of "enlightened" management. They are not accustomed to setting more radical norms which seek to change the consensus. With apologies to Lord Devlin, they are "activist" but not "dynamic" law makers. The enormous jurisdictions make the tribunals inclined to respect a wide band of "reasonable" managerial decisions'.

23 Of the cases heard in 1980, 1981, and 1982, unfair dismissal complainants in general were successful in 27.7%, 23.3%, and 30.7% of their cases. (Figures from the *Employment Gazettes* of December 1981, December 1982, and October 1983.) Complainants whose dismissal claim was joined with a claim of sex discrimination won 28%, 44%, and 30% of their hearings in those years.

24 The figures were:

	1980 %	1981 %	1982 %	Total %
Sex discrimination claims	23	23	50	31
SDA claims combined with UD/USR claims	5	19	20	15

25 These numbers are certain to be an under-estimate. DE recording procedures apparently mean that it is possible for a case to be classified as *only* 'unfair dismissal' even where there was an additional sex discrimination claim.

26 *Creagh v Speedway Sign Service,* Appeal No EAT 312/83 and *Hassan v Harlow District Council and J Ward,* Appeal No EAT 161/84.

27 Obviously, this sort of analysis cannot be considered precise, because of the possibility that evidence was presented which is not mentioned in the decision. However, a review of the decisions which followed the hearings observed during the study showed they usually *did* mention the *type* of evidence submitted, if not always its substance. Also, the use of fairly broad categories should compensate for omissions of that sort, and it is probable that a good approximation of the actual situation was attained.

28 Lustgarten (1977), p212, p220. He explains: '. . . statistical evidence will be part of both kinds of discrimination cases, but it is important to notice that its purpose and importance are decidedly different in each. Whereas the focus in direct discrimination cases is on the decisions and practices of the particular respondent, the concept of indirect discrimination requires a more global comparison – between the "posture and condition" of the relevant minority and majority populations. In the former case statistical evidence is used to undermine, or to buttress, the credibility of witnesses; it cannot of itself furnish a legal conclusion of discrimination. In the latter, statistics demonstrating disparity are *themselves* the direct evidence of what the statute proscribes. Comparative statistics thus comport precisely with the concept of indirect discrimination; in contrast, demographic statistics, which are not designed to measure the effect of any particular employment criterion, are of no value in cases of this kind'.

29 [1978] IRLR 225.

30 [1979] IRLR 316, [1980] IRLR 210.

31 Zander (1982), p236.

32 Complainants' type of representation (or lack of it) also made a difference in the outcome of the conciliation stage of cases. See Graham and Lewis, (1985).

33 Information from *Annual Reports* of the EOC for Northern Ireland.

34 On the problems of the accuracy of DE statistics and the difficulties in analysing them, see Appendix I.

35 *Annual Reports* of the EOC of England, Wales and Scotland, 1980, 1981, and 1982.

36   At the time of this study, the Industrial Tribunals (Rules of Procedure) Regulations 1980.
37   *Craig v British Railways Board* [1973] 8 ITR 636, NIRC, cited in Goodman (1979), p63.
38   Communication from tribunal chairman George McLaughlin, 20 August 1984.
39   Hepple (1983), p79.

CHAPTER 4

ADVICE AND REPRESENTATION FOR COMPLAINANTS

The fact that complainants frequently presented so little evidence to the tribunals raised the question of how they were identifying, preparing and presenting their claims. The decisions were therefore reviewed to ascertain where complainants had obtained advice, and whether particular issues were more troublesome than others. Specific consideration was given to the question whether it was primarily unrepresented complainants who had difficulty; an attempt was also made to determine whether differences existed between types of representatives. From the decisions and other sources, it was apparent that simply recognising a sex discrimination or equal pay claim, articulating it, and filing it within the existing time limit proved a problem for a considerable number of people, even those with advice or representation.

Filing Out-of-Time

Time limits exist under both the EQPA 1970 and the SDA 1975. Limits for filing equal pay claims are sufficiently generous to cause complainants few problems, if any. These allow an employee to file an application at any time during their employment, or up to six months after the employment ends.[1]

The limitations for filing sex discrimination claims are far more restrictive: an application must be filed within three months of the date of the incident which is the source of the complaint.[2] This limit causes complainants considerable problems: in fact, a remarkable number of complainants' applications were dismissed because they were out-of-time: nearly 20 individual applications were dismissed in whole or in part because the three-month limit had passed. Some missed the deadline by as little as one day; others by as much as 20 months. In two cases, the complainants were simply inexcusably late; but several others recounted to the tribunals difficulties they had encountered in obtaining advice from solicitors, a job centre, or the CAB. In fact, over half of these complainants had taken advice: from their trades unions, from the EOC, or from a solicitor. In such cases, the tribunals generally felt bound by the position that such bodies were 'skilled advisers' (even where they clearly were not) and that the three-month time limit therefore could not be waived.

Detailed accounts of the actions of the advisers involved were provided by several of these decisions. In three, where the complainant was advised by a trade union, the tribunal considered the union official involved to have been negligent. The account in one of these cases is representative: the complainant had originally filed her IT-1, 'indicating her employment had ended but giving absolutely no indication what complaint she was making or what remedy she sought'. She had indicated on the form that she was represented by the divisional organiser of her union; the form was therefore returned by COIT to him. Then followed an extended period in which the organiser failed to take action, despite two additional letters from COIT. Over nine months later, the organiser filed an application claiming the reason for the dismissal was 'sex discrimination'. The tribunal wrote:

> In spite of the submission of the form IT-1 in May 1981, it is quite apparent that no application was in fact submitted in this case until February 1982. Whatever Mrs McDonagh's own part in the matter, it is clear that the case has been handled with the most extraordinary dilatoriness in her Union office. Unfortunately for Mrs McDonagh, the Union must be regarded as 'skilled advisers' for this purpose, who must answer to her for any failure on their part to pursue her rights on her behalf. So far as the tribunal is concerned, so long as the Union were representing her, their actions are for practical purposes to be regarded as hers. Wherever the fault lies, both insofar as the application was one of unfair dismissal and insofar as it may have been on the grounds of sex discrimination, the complaint should have been lodged, at the latest, about the time the first form was sent in . . . There is nothing in the papers to indicate that there is any ground whatsoever for saying that it was 'not practicable' for the application to be submitted in time, or to show that it was in any way impracticable for it to be submitted during the ensuing nine months . . *(Mrs McDonagh v Alumsac Ltd)*

In another case, a complainant's delay clearly originated with her solicitor. She was a teacher and claimed both unfair dismissal and sex discrimination in dismissal. While her discrimination claim was recognised at the time she was dismissed, her solicitor waited until the conclusion of her union grievance procedure to file both claims with the tribunals, although this meant filing more than three months from the date of dismissal itself. The solicitor argued to the tribunal that the three-month time limitation should date from the time the union procedure concluded. The tribunal disagreed. It decided the claim for unfair dismissal, which had been filed in time, but unanimously refused to exercise its discretion to hear the late sex discrimination claim because it did not find it 'just and equitable' to do so in those circumstances (*Vera Gould v Derbyshire County Council*).

Perhaps surprisingly, in a case involving the EOC, one tribunal took a different position. The chairman stated:

> It is clear to us that the applicant was out of time in that, on her originating application, she stated that the act complained of first came to her knowledge on 6 May. She made various approaches to the Job Centre, apparently without great satisfaction, as to how she could go about making a claim before an industrial tribunal for sex discrimination. She then wrote in late June 1980 to the EOC, who replied, over four weeks later, giving advice in the following terms:
>
>> Under the Sex Discrimination Act an application to a tribunal must be made within three months of the alleged discriminatory act. In your case this would be from the date on which you received the letter confirming your termination from Contract Clean (Southern) Limited. Therefore if you wish to apply to the tribunal you should do so before 15th August 1980.
>
> It is quite clear to us that this advice is totally wrong, and that the application should have been presented before 6 August. Nevertheless, we cannot fault the applicant for accepting the advice of such a body as the EOC, and under those circumstances we consider that it is just and equitable to extend her time and to allow her case to be heard on its merits. (*Mrs Oxenbury v (1) Contract Clean (Southern) Ltd. and (2) Racal Communications Ltd.*)

Here the tribunal referred to its power under s.76(5) of the SDA 1975 to 'consider any such complaint, claim or application out of time if, in all the circumstances of the case, it considers that it is just and equitable to do so'. This discretion would appear to be substantially broader than that available in unfair dismissal cases, where the tribunal may extend the filing period if it finds it was 'not practicable' for the application to be submitted in time. In fact, the discretion available in discrimination cases would appear to include situations where complainants miss deadlines due to incorrect advice, even from otherwise 'skilled' advisers. None the less, it remained the general practice of tribunals not to extend the time limit where an individual filed late after consulting with the EOC, a union, or a solicitor.

Recognising the Discrimination or Equal Pay Claim

Unhappily, there were cases which were filed, prepared and heard by the tribunals where the parties apparently never identified the existence of a sex discrimination or equal pay claim. There were about 20 sex discrimination and equal pay cases in 1980-1982 which suggested additional sex discrimination or equal pay claims that could have been made. These included several unfair dismissal cases (usually combined with a claim for equal pay) where the facts also suggested a claim for victimisation, although this was neither claimed by the complainant nor raised by the tribunal. There was a claim of sex discrimination in dismissal where the complainant did not make what appeared to be a good claim for equal pay *(Mrs Turner v FTL Co Ltd)*. There were also at least three cases alleging direct discrimination where there seemed to be viable claims of indirect discrimination which were, again, not made. These involved informal promotion procedures *(Mrs Bell v Newcastle-upon-Tyne City Council);* a promotion system based on post-qualification experience and its equivalents *(Mrs Baker v Surrey County Council);* and selection for redundancy on the basis of skilled-time worked *(Delia O'Brien v Schreiber Furniture Ltd)*. In about one-third of these cases, the complainant was not represented; in another third, the complainant was represented by a trade union official or some other representative; and in the remainder the decision did not state whether or not the complainant was represented.

This study reviews only those cases where an equal pay or a sex discrimination claim of some description *had* been made. It is likely that there may be more of these 'missed' claims among applications which simply claim an unfair dismissal or unfair selection for redundancy. Two clear examples of this are the case of *Clark and Powell v Eley (IMI) Ltd, Kynoch Ltd.,*[3] where the complainants, claiming unfair selection for redundancy, failed to recognise a claim for *sex discrimination* in selection for redundancy until they received legal assistance; and a case characterised as an 'unfair dismissal case' with no reference whatsoever to sex discrimination, even though the complainant alleged, and the tribunal held that the dismissal had been solely because he was a man (*Mr Fice v Moods Fashions*).

Producing Necessary Evidence

The case decisions suggest an overwhelmingly frequent failure to identify correctly and obtain in advance information appropriate to support the claim and present it in the appropriate form at the tribunal hearing. The decisions repeatedly refer to this problem and others which flow from it: the failure to present relevant statistics, the failure to bring comparative evidence, the failure to bring sufficiently extensive information to prove a 'pattern' of behaviour, etc. Among the 215 decisions from 1980-1982, there were almost 50 where either the tribunal specifically described some failure of the complainant or their representative, or where it was reasonably apparent that insufficient information had been offered on the complainant's behalf. In general, these problems occurred where complainants were unrepresented, or where they were represented by trade union officials or other lay representatives.

Evidence from Witnesses
Ten tribunals dismissed cases where complainants brought no corroborating witnesses or brought witnesses whose testimony was unhelpful. Another half-dozen mentioned the failure of complainants to obtain information from the respondents' witnesses, usually as a result of ineffective cross-examination. In all of these cases where the type of representation was stated in the decision the complainant was unrepresented or had non-legal representation.

Written Statements
There were several cases where complainants had brought written statements to substitute for the testimony of live witnesses, only to be informed by the tribunal that the statements were virtually worthless. In almost all of the 10 cases where written statements were rejected, the complainants were represented by trades union officials and lay representatives, not by legally trained representatives.

Basic and Comparative Evidence
A number of decisions dismissed the complainants' sex discrimination claim stating that they had brought 'no evidence' to support

them. There were another dozen cases where the complainant or their representative apparently failed to present necessary comparative evidence. Of these decisions, over half did not indicate whether the complainant was represented; three stated they were not represented; and three stated they were represented without stating the type of representation.

Statistical Evidence
There were also notable instances where complainants and/or their representatives failed to present necessary statistical evidence. A few tribunals noted specifically the lack of relevant and convincing statistical evidence in cases they decided, including one application alleging department-wide discrimination in promotions and two alleging indirect discrimination. In others the lack of necessary statistical evidence was obvious. In most of these cases, the complainants were represented by trades union officials or other lay persons.

Claims Not Pursued at the Hearing
There were several cases where the sex discrimination claim was not pursued at the hearing; most were cases where the complainant claimed unfair dismissal and also included the claim of sex discrimination. Decisions stated, for example, 'the discrimination claim never figured in this case', 'there was no evidence submitted about sex discrimination', 'the applicants agreed not to pursue the discrimination claim', and 'her representatives did not press the claim of discrimination'. In some of these cases complainants had representatives; in a few, they did not. There are occasions where a decision not to pursue a claim can certainly be an appropriate one. Without further information it is impossible to conclude whether these particular decisions resulted from a lack of expertise, either in making the sex discrimination claim in the first instance, or in pursuing it and presenting it to the tribunal. However at least a few of the claims which were not pursued appeared likely, on the facts that were stated, to have had some merit.

Presenting Claims

It was also apparent that quite significant numbers of lay individuals encountered difficulties in preparing and presenting sex discrimination and equal pay claims to the tribunals. Many had trouble 'conducting' the hearing. For example, at every hearing where there was an unrepresented party or parties, they had difficulty with cross-examination. Two, after attempting cross-examination and being 'instructed' by the chairman, gave up and did not proceed to try to cross-examine a respondent or respondent's witnesses – even though they felt the individual had not told the truth and they knew it was important to 'force it out'. Self-represented respondents tended to give long, discursive narratives, usually to the irritation of the tribunal. A few individuals even had trouble eliciting testimony from their own witnesses. One respondent's witness observed had a very awkward time while her employer tried to 'question' her. When interviewed later, she said:

> They shouldn't have asked him to ask me the questions, it was stupid. The Chairman had heard him speak, so he knew what the questions would be. He should have asked them himself.

Several unrepresented parties spontaneously expressed the need for more information about the hearing. The most articulate and able unrepresented respondent observed stated:

> At the start, the chairman should explain the procedure – who goes first, etc. He should tell you to take notes if you've got something to say, rather than waiting until you try to interrupt and then scolding you. It made me feel like a schoolboy . . . It was disturbing that unsworn letters were not adequate. It's a breakdown in communication – ACAS told us that bringing a letter was fine . . . I did not expect a normal law court, but the chairman acted as though it were one. I thought it would be more informal, relaxed, and that you would get more help and guidance.

Observations made in this study do not support the obvious idea that a clear explanation of the procedure provided by the chairman at the start of a hearing would eliminate some of these problems. In fact, in the one instance where the chairman *did* explain the order the hearing would follow, both parties later said that they had not understood him. These are clearly serious and considerable problems; in fact they are often referred to by chairmen, both in their decisions and in discussion, and they occurred without exception at every hearing observed where one party or the other was unrepresented or had a representative who was not legally trained.

Advice and Assistance to Complainants

The above examples strongly suggest that the availability and use of representation does not necessarily eliminate the problems complainants face in filing sex discrimination and equal pay claims. Mistakes in filing claims, recognising claims, and presenting them to the tribunal occurred frequently in cases handled by lay and trades union representatives and even, in a few cases, with legal representation. The cases in which complainants or respondents were clearly illadvised included one involving ACAS, one with the EOC, five with job centres, and four with different trades unions.

Job Centres

During the three-year period reviewed, 11 tribunal decisions referred to a job centre. In four of these, the job centre had been helpful to the complainant, either by correcting an employer's discriminatory actions in the first instance, by directing the complainant to the EOC for advice, or by actually attending the tribunal hearing and testifying on the complainant's behalf. However, the other seven cases raise certain concerns. In a few, the job centre had honoured an employer's traditional divisions between male and female employees or their requests for applicants of one sex only;[4] and in two cases, the job centre was the respondent. In one case where the respondent was the job centre the tribunal found it *had* discriminated. The complainant, a young man, had inquired about an advert at the job centre, only to be told by the receptionist that there were vacancies for female applicants only. In the course of the hearing on this case, it became clear both that the centre receptionist had undergone no training on these issues and that the acting manager of the centre held a wholly inaccurate understanding of the law. The tribunal concluded:

> We accept that the receptionist may not have immediately appreciated that what she was doing was discriminatory and unlawful. We think, however, that the training of a receptionist for job centre work should be of such nature as to alert an officer in that position at least sufficiently to put to her superior any instructions received from an employer of the kind which she says she received. We would also have expected a more senior employee such as the acting manager to recognise a so-called quota system as between men and women for applications for a particular job, as unlawful. If a quota operates, even on a 50-50 basis, it means that at some

stage when the quota allotted to applicants of one sex has been filled any further applicant of that sex will be refused the opportunity of going forward for the job merely on account of that applicant's sex. *(Mr Jones v (1) Lovell and Christmas Ltd and (2) Manpower Services Commission)*

It is worth noting the manager's own explanation: he had consulted ACAS on the question and been told that quota systems 'were a grey area'.

One Scottish tribunal also identified a situation in which a job centre had incorrectly advised an employer that in a particular situation they could legally advertise for and hire only women *(Mr Curran v Scottish Episcopal Theological College)*.

Trades Unions

A surprising number of tribunals criticised representation by trades union officers. These comments referred both to the actual advice given and presentation of the case, and to important conflicts between the claims of the complainants and the positions of their trades unions.

Advice and Case Presentation

As indicated in Chapter 3, tribunals faulted union representatives for providing incorrect advice on filing dates (several cases); for incorrect advice on the nature of the claim; and for failing to bring and present to the tribunal relevant evidence on necessary points (several cases). There were other miscellaneous criticisms where there was union representation, including one case where the representative was unable to specify the particular breach of the SDA 1975 alleged. In another case a trade union representative – having refused to attend a preliminary hearing or discussion on an equal pay case – then requested permission at the hearing to substitute the name of a wholly different male comparator to the complainant.

Conflicts of Interest

A more serious problem reflected in the decisions involved instances in which the complainants' position conflicted with those of their unions. For example, in one case several women claimed sex discrimination in their selection for redundancy. Four of them were represented by a legal officer of their union. It was shown at the hearing that there was a traditional division of the respondent's workforce by sex, and that the union branch, and the workforce generally, were positively in favour of this sex-based job demarcation. On occasions the union branch had objected to proposals to train women for jobs previously done by men. The tribunal remarked:

> . . . it must be said that the claim of sex discrimination by the four applicants represented by (the union deputy legal officer) have not been very vigorously pursued – understandably perhaps, because the branch of his union at the respondents' undertaking has (to say the least) gone along with the situation which is now claimed to have been discriminatory. In saying that, we wish to make it quite clear that we do not suggest that the union nationally or regionally is other than wholly committed in theory and in practice to a policy of equal opportunities, whatever may have been the general attitude of the membership of the local branch. (The union deputy legal officer) in this matter has been in rather a difficult position. *(Mrs Grace (and seven others) v Kraft Foods Ltd)*

Other decisions noted that the contested wage structure of the redundancy procedure which was being challenged had been agreed by the complainant's union. A number of others pointedly documented individual lapses by union stewards in their roles with the complainants. For example, one tribunal wrote:

> The respondents enquired through the applicant's shop steward whether the applicant was interested in a lower grade position in another department and received the qualified reply from the shop steward that she was prepared to give it a trial . . . The respondents decided that they were not prepared to make such an offer and informed the shop steward accordingly who despite being asked repeatedly by the applicant what the position was, did not inform her of the respondents' decisions . . .

> Having heard all the evidence the tribunal took the view that the applicant was fully entitled to present her complaint, but that if her shop steward had had the moral courage to keep her properly informed as he should have done, then the necessity of making the complaint would not have arisen. *(Mrs Wallwork v Brytallium Castings (Bolton) Ltd)*

The review of the 215 decisions revealed five cases where there was entrenched and active workforce and/or union opposition to the complainant's position (usually in the form of job demarcations by sex); several cases where the complainant's claim for equal pay or unfair selection for redundancy ran counter to a union-agreed or supported wage structure or redundancy procedure; and another five where particular actions of union stewards or other officials, either before redundancy or at the hearing, were directly contrary to the complainants' interests. In several cases, the conflict between the complainant's claim and the union position resulted in the complainant being unrepresented; in others it simply meant that the representative had the awkward task of propounding a position that was counter to union policy.

The Overall Picture

This by no means suggests that all union representatives did an inadequate job of pursuing sex discrimination claims. In at least one decision, involving a union legal officer, the tribunal's comments were laudatory. It nevertheless seems an inescapable observation that representation by the trades unions was not in general an adequate answer for sex discrimination and equal pay complainants during the years studied.

This is consistent with the findings of a recent study of ACAS conciliation in sex discrimination and equal pay cases, which makes the following observations on trade union advice and representation:

> In the interview, applicants' attitudes towards trades unions divided sharply between those who thought that they had received admirable service and those who were very unflattering. Those who were most complimentary about their unions tended to be in unions or branches which catered more for women than men. Some were fulsome about the help they had received, saying it was the only real source of help that they had and that they could never have managed without it. At the other extreme we interviewed several applicants who alleged that their trades unions were in league with the employer. Several others remarked that their shop stewards or officials had been very enthusiastic at the outset, but less so as time wore on, even to the extent of performing a total volte-face at the end.

> The ACAS officers whom we interviewed felt that trades unions' support was very uneven. In general they felt that the traditional blue-collar unions tended to be less sympathetic than some of the new white-collar unions, a point which

other commentators have also made, and which receives some support from our interviews with trades unions' representatives. As to applicants' allegations that unions were 'in league with employers', we became convinced in three of the 45 cases which we discussed with ACAS officers, that the trades unions or shop stewards had been largely responsible either for women withdrawing their claims or for the woman losing her case at tribunal.

It may be that union culture accounts for some variation in the quality of representation provided to applicants, but clearly another major factor is the difficulty which most union representatives have in dealing with the complexities of the legislation. None of the representatives whom we interviewed had much experience of equal pay and sex discrimination matters, and they did not seem to have a thorough grasp, for example, of the intricacies of establishing an indirect discrimination claim, or the complications of European Community legislation. One point on which all were agreed was the evidential difficulty of proving a case of equal pay or sex discrimination.

At national level, some unions have shown an impressive response to equal opportunity issues, others less so. However, at local level, the picture which emerged was one of representatives who were not particularly sensitive to equal opportunity issues, who had very little direct contact with the EOC, and who had a less than thorough grasp of the legislation. An additional difficulty they face is that sex discrimination and equal pay cases can and do come into conflict with established trade union policies, such as agreed redundancy schemes. Whilst the solution obviously is to draw up policies which are non-discriminatory, it has to be recognised that as long as such conflicts do exist, local union representatives are likely to resolve them in favour of existing collective procedures.

Although unions have a vital role to play in the promotion of equal opportunities, we do not think it is realistic to expect them to be a major source of support for tribunal applicants. First, the law in this area is tremendously complicated and specialist advisers are required. Given their wide range of concerns we have substantial doubts about the unions' ability to provide such specialist advice, especially at the local level. Secondly, around half of all applicants in equal pay and sex discrimination cases are not union members at all.[5]

The Equal Opportunities Commission

The case decisions reflected a few problems encountered by complainants who had consulted the EOC. For example, in a number of cases, complainants failed to file their applications on time even though they had had advice from the EOC. One woman had posted her application on the last possible day, but *to the EOC*; by the time it was forwarded by the EOC to the tribunal office it was, of course, past the filing deadline. The tribunal held she had received 'skilled advice' and refused to extend the time limit *(Miss Belinda Power v Berni Inns Ltd)*. In another case, a woman employed by the National Coal Board's television unit filed a sex discrimination complaint related to her dismissal. She took advice from the EOC, but none the less subsequently filed her application *one day after the deadline.* The tribunal noted the EOC had been involved and said:

> (The complainant) can give no explanation for her failure to post her application to the Central Office of the Industrial Tribunals within time other than that she had taken on a new job and was under a lot of pressure there and was giving most of her time to that job. *(Miss McGlinchey v National Coal Board)*

It dismissed the application as out-of-time.

In a third case a woman doctor had filed an equal pay application that she sought to amend at the hearing to include a claim of sex discrimination. Although the respondents did not raise any objections, the tribunal nevertheless refused to permit the amendment, referring to the fact that the complainant had been given advice on her case from the EOC:

> All the facts on which the applicant relied in her claim under the Sex Discrimination Act were known to her when she retired from her employment, and she was also receiving advice from the Equal Opportunities Commission. Had the complaint been made at the same time as her complaint under the Equal Pay Act which was in June 1981 it would still have been out of time but the tribunal would also certainly have allowed an extension. In all the circumstances, however, the tribunal do not consider it would be just and equitable to allow an extension until today and the tribunal therefore refuse the application to include a complaint under the Sex Discrimination Act . . (*D J W Cuthbert v May and Baker Ltd*)

From these excerpts it is not clear whether the fault lies with the EOC. It is certainly possible that in each instance the EOC gave correct advice about filing deadlines but the complainant simply failed to follow it. The information does, however, at the very least suggest that identifying and filing by the relevant deadlines present some difficulties, even where complainants have informed advice.

A second problem reflected by the cases reviewed is the delay complainants experienced in receiving advice from the EOC and in the appointment of a legal representative. A number of decisions referred to this. The decision on one case where the complainant filed late, noted it had taken the EOC four weeks to respond to the complainant's inquiry *(Mrs Oxenbury v (1) Contract Clean (Southern) Ltd and (2) Racal Communications Ltd)*. In another case the complainant had waited 'some time' before receiving advice from the EOC, but his application was none the less filed within the statutory time limit *(Mr Court v EMI Film and Theatre Corp Ltd)*. In these two instances the EOC delay did not actually prejudice the complainant in any way. In two other cases, however, tribunals were clearly upset at late requests for hearing postponements which were due to the EOC designating solicitors so close to the hearing date that adequate preparation was impossible *(Mrs Grace-Walsh v Andrew Page Ltd; Mr K Torr v Burgerfair)*. In one case the tribunal granted the request for a postponement. In the other, where the request for postponement was received only two days before the hearing date, the tribunal refused the application and expressed its criticism:

> The EOC should know by this time that the tribunal realises that this kind of case does often require more preparation than some and that, so far as the tribunal in (this region) is concerned, there is generally no difficulty in obtaining a deferment of listing or a postponement if made in reasonable time before the date fixed. On the other hand tribunals when fixed sometimes cannot be cancelled on sort notice without expenditure which may run into hundreds of pounds. It was the unanimous view of the tribunal that this application for postponement was far too late and it was refused, subject to the qualification that, if the tribunal should feel that there were any real difficulties as the case proceeded, they would reconsider the matter. *(Mrs Grace-Walsh v Andrew Page Ltd)*

Other problems were mentioned by parties in the cases observed. The two complainants who eventually received financial support for representation from the EOC found the initial period of communicating with the EOC 'long distance' (by telephone or by letter) distressing. This complaint should not be regarded as frivolous: these complainants were both independent, capable women, and one had received assistance from her local CAB (which itself expressed frustration at having to deal with the EOC by post and long-distance telephone calls). It seems that the fact that the EOC has only a single, centralised office in Manchester does create problems for complainants which should be considered and addressed. In addition, the initial contact which both these complainants had with the EOC employment section led them to believe that representation at the tribunal hearing was assured – only to be alarmed later to learn that requests for assistance must be placed formally before the Commissioners. In these two cases, legal support was eventually approved, but in both cases, the solicitors engaged by the EOC were forced to prepare their cases in an extremely short period of time. This is apparently not a frequent problem but, even so, it would be useful for the EOC to consider ways to minimise the frequency with which it does occur. It is important to note that these complainants were ultimately impressed and completely satisfied with the legal representation they received through the EOC, and indeed the EOC-appointed representatives' presentations at the hearings were exceptionally able.

The Regional Offices of Industrial Tribunals

The industrial tribunals are empowered to contact complainants about the substance of their claims in two situations:

(1) Where the Secretary of the Tribunals is of the opinion that the originating application does not seek or on the facts stated therein cannot entitle the applicant to a relief which a tribunal has power to give, he may give notice to that effect to the applicant stating the reasons for his opinion and informing him that the application will not be registered unless he states in writing that he wishes to proceed with it (Rule 1(1),(2)).

and

(2) A tribunal may . . . of its own motion (i) require a party to furnish in writing to the person specified by the tribunal further particulars of the grounds on which he or it relies and of any facts and contentions relevant thereto . . (Rule 4(1)(b)(i)).

116

This study was primarily concerned with decisions reached after hearings and so case decisions in instances such as these were not methodically collected. Even so, there were several in the three-year period examined. In at least two of these, unrepresented complainants were wholly incapable of responding in a meaningful way to requests for particulars of their claims. They did not respond within time limits set by the tribunals and showed considerable confusion about tribunal procedures and the relationship of other advisory bodies to the proceedings *(Miss Stonier v Byatts of Fenton Ltd; Mr Martin v Metropolitan Police)*. In both cases, their inadequate responses eventually led to the dismissal of their applications. Other cases occurred where the ROIT dealt with complainants' designated representatives.Unfortunately, this situation by no means meant fewer difficulties. For example, in one case, a regional office received an application that 'gave absolutely no indication of what complaint she was making or what remedy she sought'. It returned the application to the trade union organiser named by the complainant as her representative. Although the office sent two reminder letters, the official did not forward a completed form to the ROIT until over eight months later. It was dismissed by the tribunal which reviewed it as out of time, although it appeared that all of this may well have transpired without the knowledge of the complainant *(Mrs McDonagh v Alumsac Ltd)*.

In cases such as these, the regional offices are undertaking the difficult task of providing and eliciting information about legal matters; the task is complicated by the fact that they are communicating by letter, and by the tribunals' need to maintain impartiality. This seems a particularly unsatisfactory situation which is both inefficient and frustrating to all involved.

Notes

1   EQPA 1970,s.2(3).
2   SDA 1975, s.76(1). For a more detailed discussion, see Chapter 3.
3   [1982] IRLR 131, [1982] IRLR 482.
4   In one case, the complanaint claimed the Job Centre receptionist discouraged her from applying for a job as a driver/salesperson for a meat factory because two women had actually been sent and had been refused (this allegaton was not proven) *(Mrs McEwan v George Hopkins Ltd)*. In the second, the complainant claimed that when the job centre clerk telephoned an employer to arrange an interview for him, she was told – and accepted without question - that the employers wanted a girl *(Mr Jarvis v (1) Southend M.O.T. Test Centre and (2) Manpower Services Commission)*.

5   Graham and Lewis (1985). A team at the Centre for Criminological and Socio-Legal Studies at the University of Sheffield, using cases from three regions (Yorkshire and Humberside, the Midlands, and the North West), collected 164 completed questionnaires from complainants and respondents; interviewed 45 complainants and 34 respondents, and discussed 45 cases with ACAS officers.

CHAPTER 5

SUCCESS AT HEARINGS: A STATISTICAL ANALYSIS

The reasons a particular legal claim prevails or fails are both complicated and elusive. However, by measuring success rates during the three-year period studied against several variables, it is possible to identify certain circumstances or institutional conditions which tend to increase a complainant's ability to produce sufficient, appropriate evidence to establish her case. Several aspects of the 215 sex discrimination and equal pay cases decided in England and Wales in 1980-1982 were analysed to see whether they related to case outcome, including various characteristics of the complainants and respondents; certain administratively-controlled factors such as the composition of the tribunal panels; and certain aspects of the hearings themselves, including type of representation, number of witnesses used by the complainant and the length of the hearing. A few of the more important variables were examined in more detail. Where information on hearings in Scotland was reliable and useful, it was also included.

The Complainants

In the three-year period studied, men had a somewhat higher success rate on their claims (32%) than women (26%). Moreover, equal pay claims were generally more successful (29%) than sex discrimination claims (26%). However, an analysis by type of claim revealed certain interesting differences, both in the types of claims brought by the different sexes and in their success.[1]

Table 5.1   *Complainants' success at SDA and EQPA hearings 1980-1982, by type of discrimination alleged and complainant's sex*

	Total no of claims	Men		Women	
Type of claim		No of claims	Success %	No of claims	Success %
Sex discrimination claims:					
Recruitment, Hiring	40	23	43	17	41

119

Table 5.1 *(Cont.)*

Promotion, Transfer	30	2	0	28	28
Dismissal	53	8	25	45	22
Victimisation	10	0	–	10	10
Other	29	6	17	23	9
Total	162	39	33	123	23
Equal pay claims:					
Grading scheme	17	0	–	17	18
Other	55	8	12	47	36
Total	72	8	12	64	31

It is immediately apparent that an overall success rate for sex discrimination claims obscures quite significant variation in the successes of different types of claims: claims of discrimination in recruitment were quite successful, for both men and women; claims of sex discrimination in dismissal distinctly less so; and claims of victimisation largely unsuccessful. With equal pay claims, those involving grading schemes were distinctly less successful than all other types of equal pay claims. And for certain types of claims, success rates were quite different for men and women.

In unfair dismissal cases (for the years 1980-1982), out of the total number of complainants who took unfair dismissal claims through to tribunal hearings, 27% were successful.

Complainants' Occupations

Table 5.2 provides the figures for success by complainants' occupations in the three-year period examined.

Table 5.2 *Complainants' success at SDA and EQPA hearings 1980-1982, by complainants' occupation*

	SDA claims		EQPA claims	
		Success		Success
	No	%	No	%
Professional/Managerial	48	15	16	31
Clerical, Related	27	37	19	16
Sales	17	29	8	50
All Manual	59	27	25	32
Total	151	25	68	29

Complainants in manual jobs fared nearly as well with sex discrimination as with equal pay claims. In all other job categories, complainants' success rates under the two different Acts were quite different.

Certain changes occurred over the three-year period. In 1980 and 1981 sex discrimination claims by complainants in professional/managerial occupations had a very low success rate. Even with their very much higher rate in 1982, these cases had by far the lowest overall success rate. This may reflect a tendency among tribunals to permit greater discretion to employers in the selection and promotion of individuals for professional and high managerial positions.[2] Sex discrimination cases brought by complainants in clerical and clerical-related occupations increased in both number and the rate of success. The opposite trend prevailed with respect to equal pay claims: the rate of success fell in cases brought by complainants of all occupations except professional/managerial. In fact, in 1982 there was not a single successful claim brought by complainants in clerical or selling occupations.[3]

Multiple-Complainant Cases

It seemed possible that cases with more than one complainant might have a higher rate of success, whether because a greater body of facts might be made available to the tribunal or because the greater 'presence' might assist the complainant's case. However, the review conducted revealed that cases involving more than one complainant were *not* consistently more or less successful than others.[4] In fact, with sex discrimination cases, the pattern reversed completely between 1980 and 1982: originally, joint claims by two complainants succeeded twice as often (33%) as did those by single complainants (17%). In 1982, however, claims by single complainants succeeded twice as often (41%) as those with two complainants (20%). With equal pay cases, there was no evidence that cases with multiple complainants succeeded more frequently.

The Respondents[5]

The information gained from the decisions on the type of the respondents permitted only a basic breakdown between 'government' respondents (central and local and government, and nationalised industries) and those which were registered companies. The analysis showed that 80% of hearings in which 'government' respondents were involved between 1980-1982 were resolved in favour of the respondents; whereas registered companies won about 70% of the hearings against them.

Aspects of the Tribunal Hearings

The 215 hearing decisions were reviewed to determine the length of the hearings, the type of chairman presiding, whether the panel included a woman, and whether witnesses were presented by the parties. In each instance, this information was cross-tabulated with case outcome.

Full-Time Chairmen

As noted in Chapter 3, in 1980-1982, full-time chairmen heard only two-thirds of the sex discrimination claims and only half of the equal pay claims; all others were heard by part-time chairmen. Throughout the three-year period, complainants heard by full-time chairmen had a higher rate of success (32%) than complainants heard by part-time chairmen (22%). In 1982 the success rate with full-time chairmen was *twice* that with part-time chairmen (42% versus 21%).[6] The figures were somewhat more extreme for equal pay claims than for sex discrimination claims.

Table 5.3 *Complainants' success at SDA and EQPA hearings 1980-1982, by type of tribunal chairman*

	SDA Claims Heard	Success %	EQPA Claims Heard	Success %
Full-time Chairmen	99	28	34	38
Part-time Chairmen	49	20	36	19

Women on Tribunal Panels

As noted in Chapter 3, tribunal panels included a woman in 92% of sex discrimination claims and 77% of equal pay claims. The percentage of panels including a woman decreased each year during the period studied. Panels which included a woman did decide in the complainant's favour more often than all-male panels. In fact, overall, male and female complainants won twice as often when their panel included a woman member than when the panel was all-male (30% versus 14%).[7] The difference was slightly greater for equal pay claims than for claims of sex discrimination.

Table 5.4 *Complainants' success at SDA and EQPA hearings 1980-1982, by composition of tribunal panel*

	SDA Claims Heard	Success %	EQPA Claims Heard	Success %
Women on the panel	136	26	54	33
All-male panel	12	17	16	12

Scotland

In Scotland, where the tribunal panel included a woman and a full-time chairman in every sex discrimination and equal pay claim, there was a 42% success rate for the period 1980-1982.

Parties' Use of Witnesses

Complainants

Complainants who presented witnesses had distinctly higher rates of success at tribunal hearings, with success increasing dramatically for sex discrimination complainants.

Table 5.5 *Complainants' success at SDA and EQPA hearings 1980-1982, by complainant's use of witnesses*

	Total	Complainant only		One witness		Two witnesses		Three or more witnesses	
	No	No	Won %	No	Won %	No	Won %	No	Won %
SDA Claims	148	108	17	22	50	9	78	9	22
EQPA Claims	70	49	29	12	33	3	33	6	33

With sex discrimination claims, cases where one witness was presented were three times as successful as those where only the complainant testified; where two witnesses were presented, success increased four times. For equal pay claims, complainants who presented witnesses won somewhat more frequently than at hearings where only the complainant testified. However, the difference was far less dramatic. While it may seem only common sense that more witnesses will mean a greater likelihood of success since the tribunal is presented with a fuller, more convincing story, the difference revealed here is nevertheless extraordinary. It seems likely that the complainants who presented witnesses also had knowledgeable advice in preparing their case or good representation, which itself could explain the greater success achieved.

Respondents

The picture for respondents was neither so remarkable nor so consistent. In 1980 and 1981 respondents who presented only the testimony of one person were successful more often than those who presented additional witnesses. Yet in 1982, respondents, like complainants, showed greater success rates in cases where more than one person testified. However, the relative increase 'per witness' for respondents was quite small – certainly nowhere near the tremendous increase shown with respect to complainants:

respondents won from 68% - 83% of their cases regardless of the number of witnesses they used.

Length of Hearings

From 1980-1982 the tribunals decided on sex discrimination and equal pay cases in increasingly shorter hearings: in 1980, only about half the hearings were completed in one day; by 1982, three-quarters were completed in that time. This latter figure appears to be similar to that for unfair dismissal hearings, 80% of which, during the same period, were completed in one day.[8] Over the three-year period, success rates at one-day and two-day hearings were identical.[9] Thus, hearing length did not appear to have an important relationship to complainant success.

Complainants' Representation

By 1980-1982, the number of sex discrimination and equal pay claims heard by the tribunals had decreased dramatically. Therefore, to obtain the most accurate view of the relative success gained with the various types of representatives, their performance was analysed over the entire eight-year period for which statistics were available, i.e. 1976-1983.[10] During this period, the tribunals decided 717 applications under the SDA 1975 and 2,147 under the EQPA 1970. The success rates of these applications by type of representative were:

Table 5.6 *Complainants' success at SDA and EQPA 1976-1983, by type of representation*

	SDA (717)	EQPA (2147)
	%	%
Solicitor, Counsel	39	25
Trade Union	19	30
Self	21	25
Other	34	38
Representative not present	13	0
Type of representation not known	18	2

Source: DE Statistics, Tables 2(g) and 10(G)

These statistics have a severe limitation when taken as a reflection of representatives' success in that they reflect numbers of *applications* rather than number of *cases*. For example, where a representative handled a case for 40 or 50 complainants, the success rate of the type of representative would be affected quite substantially by the case outcome, much more than the success or loss by the same representative of a case for one or two individuals. Particularly among equal pay complainants, and particularly during the early years of the legislation, such multiple-complainant cases were quite frequent. Because they were often handled by trades union representatives, the figures relating to the success of those representatives can be regarded as providing a reliable indication only of the number of *complainants* whose cases were won: it is impossible to say that they reflect a real 'success rate' for trades union representatives in the normal sense of 'the number of *hearings* won compared to the total number of *hearings*'. The multiple-complainant case phenomenon may also have affected the success ratings of other types of representatives, but that impact was likely to be minor.

This study focuses primarily upon tribunal hearings. However, a representative's success in handling a tribunal application can be viewed in broader terms: certain representative groups obtained very high numbers of settlements, in which complainants received some compensation; others had a very high percentage of withdrawals. An analysis of the same DE statistics was used to analyse the success of different types of representatives in the broader sense.[11]

Sex Discrimination Applications

Complainants with legally qualified representatives were more successful than any other group, winning 39% of all cases taken to hearings and settling 28% of the applications. However, 22% of the complainants with legal representation withdrew their applications. Those who were self-represented, including those whose 'representatives were not present at the hearing', were far less successful: over 40% withdrew their applications and at hearings only 21% were successful. Trades union representatives had a somewhat worse record: although over half of the complainants represented by trades union officials went to hearings less than one-fifth were successful, a lower rate than among those with no representation. Only 17% of all complainants with trades union representation reached settlements, while 30% withdrew their applications. These figures, however, no doubt include at least a few multiple-complainant cases and should therefore be treated with caution. Complainants with representatives listed as 'other' – including individuals from CAB, relatives, or friends – did nearly as well at hearings, winning 34% of their claims; however, they had a high rate of withdrawals (39%).

Equal Pay Claims

Complainants with legally qualified representatives were very successful: only 18% withdrew their applications; 16% obtained settlements; and one-quarter of the 65% who went to hearings were successful. Self-represented complainants had a very high withdrawal rate (45%); although of the 30% who went to hearings, 25% were successful. Figures on trades union representation in equal pay cases are very greatly affected by multiple-complainant cases. Therefore, although the settlement rate is low (15%), withdrawals high (40%), and success at tribunal hearings relatively high (30%), it is impossible to know how closely these figures reflect union representatives' success *by cases*. Complainants with 'other' representatives were the most successful at hearings: 38% succeeded. However, 36% of this group withdrew their applications.

Due to the limitations of DE statistics, other sources of information are drawn on in an attempt to determine complainant success rates with different types of representatives.

Cases with Unequal Representation

The review of the 215 decisions yielded 70 decisions where the type of representation for *both* parties could be determined. These included two interesting groups: one, of 58 cases, where the respondent was represented by a solicitor or by counsel, and another, of 33 cases, where the complainant was not represented or had a lay representative (husband, father, CAB). Table 5.7 shows the success of rates of these groups.

Table 5.7   *Complainants' success at SDA and EQPA hearings 1980-1982, by the parties' relative types of representation*

No of cases	Complainant representation	Respondent representation	Complainant success rate %
24	Legal	Legal	46
13	Trade Union	Legal	38
13	Self	Legal	23
4	Husband, father, friend	Legal	0
4	CAB, Law Centre, etc.	Legal	0
10	Self	Manager	30
2	Self	Employers' Association Adviser	0

This information certainly seems to offer support for the idea that the *kind* of representation influences case outcome; in almost every instance, the more 'lay' the applicant's representative, the lower was the success rate.

EOC-Assisted Cases

Complainants who had EOC-assisted representation won 25% of their cases in 1980, 43% of their cases in 1981, and 53% of their cases in 1982. The success rate over the entire period was 41% (of a total of 41 cases). Three of the six EOC-assisted cases in Scotland from 1980-1982 were successful.

Legal Representation

Among cases where complainants had legal representation, there was a clear difference in success between those who had EOC assistance and those who did not. Of EOC-assisted cases with legal representatives, 44% were successful over the three years studied; other legal representatives were successful in 24% of cases. This difference may be explained in part by the fact that the EOC is somewhat selective in the cases it chooses to support.

Respondents' Representation

There was no information available to us which indicated relative success rates by respondents' type of representation. The tribunal decisions were thus referred to as a source of information. They showed success rates in sex discrimination and equal pay hearings handled by lawyers from 1980-1982 at 87% and 62%, respectively, and by respondents' own management, at 71% and 58% respectively. However, since almost 50% of the decisions do not provide information on the respondents' representation, these figures cannot be taken as fully reliable; if anything, they suggest a very high respondent success rate with all types of representation. It should be said that because the burden of proof on these cases lies with the complainant, respondents' high success rates may have as much to do with *failures* on the part of complainants and their representatives as with any particular successes of the respondents' representatives.

An Analysis of Success

It has already been shown that at both sex discrimination and equal pay hearings in the years 1980-1982:
(1) complainants heard by full-time chairmen were more often successful than those heard by part-time chairmen:

127

(2) complainants were more often successful before panels which included a woman than before all-male panels;

(3) complainants who presented testimony by witnesses were more often successful than those who merely testified themselves: dramatically so in cases involving sex discrimination claims.

There are several reasons why these three factors could increase a complainant's likelihood of success. For example, a woman panel member might be more willing to accept the possibility that discrimination has occurred. In addition, the interviews have suggested that the presence of a woman on the panel may make a female complainant feel more relaxed, and so improve her presentation of her case. With respect to the type of chairman, it is generally thought that full-time chairmen have greater expertise than those who are only part-time. The fact that a complainant presents supportive witnesses may indicate a stronger case and will usually mean a wider range of evidence for the tribunal. The presentation of witnesses may also indicate that the complainant has had knowledgeable representation: a factor which, as already noted, appears to have a direct relation to success.

In this section the analysis is taken a stage further, through an assessment of the relationship between these variables, combined, and success. Sex discrimination and equal pay hearings were analysed separately, which revealed that the relative importance of the three factors differs between the two types of cases. There was not suffcient evidence for either type of case to allow 'representation' to be included as a separate variable in the analysis. The sample therefore includes those cases where it could be established from the written decision whether or not there was a full-time chairman, whether there was a woman present on the panel, and the number of witnesses a complainant presented.

Sex Discrimination Claims

Table 5.8 summarises the analysis of success at hearings on sex discrimination claims.

Table 5.8 *Complainants' success at SDA hearings 1980-1982, by type of chairman, panel composition, and use of witnesses*

Panel composition	Total Cases		Complainant only		One witness		2 or more witnesses	
	%	No	%	No	%	No	%	No
1 Full-time chairman	28	(99)	21	(72)	50	(14)	46	(13)
2 Part-time chairman	21	(49)	8	(36)	50	(8)	60	(5)
3 Full-time chairman & woman	28	(92)	19	(67)	50	(14)	55	(11)
4 Part-time chairman & woman	23	(44)	14	(35)	50	(6)	67	(3)

128

Table 5.8 (cont.)

	%	No	%	No	%	No	%	No
5 Full-time chairman, no woman	29	(7)	40	(5)	–	(0)	0	(2)
4 Part-time chairman, no woman	0	(5)	0	(4)	–	(0)	0	(1)

The number of cases in each category is given in parentheses.

A comparison of lines 1 and 2 demonstrates that complainants heard by full-time chairmen had a somewhat higher success rate than those heard by part-time chairmen. Lines 3 and 4 suggest that this difference was not influenced by the presence of a woman on the panel, though in view of the small number of all-male panels this cannot be regarded as conclusive. A comparison of the columns indicating success in cases with different numbers of witnesses clearly reveals a positive and strong correlation between presenting supportive witnesses and complainant success. The presence of witnesses, rather than the number, appears to be the important factor.

An examination of the different success rates across the columns of the table and their comparison with the different success rates within and among the three pairs of lines, suggests that the key variable is the presence of witnesses, the presence of a full-time chairman being of lesser importance. The importance of having a woman on the panel could not be definitely established.

Equal Pay Claims

Table 5.9 summarises the analysis of success at hearings on equal pay claims.

Table 5.9 *Complainants' success at EQPA hearings 1980-1982, by type of chairman, panel composition, and use of witnesses*

Panel composition	Totals		Complainants only		One witness		2 or more witnesses	
	%	No	%	No	%	No	%	No
1 Full-time chairman	38	(34)	35	(23)	43	(7)	50	(4)
2 Part-time chairman	19	(36)	23	(26)	20	(5)	0	(5)
3 Full-time chairman & woman	40	(30)	38	(21)	40	(5)	50	(4)
4 Part-time chairman & woman	25	(24)	33	(18)	0	(3)	0	(3)
5 Full-time chairman, no woman	25	(4)	0	(2)	50	(2)	–	(0)
4 Part-time chairman, no woman	8	(12)	13	(8)	0	(2)	0	(2)

The number of cases in each category is given in parentheses.

First, it is clear that complainants heard by full-time chairmen had a substantially higher success rate than those heard by part-time chairmen, whether or not there was a woman on the panel. However, comparing lines 3 and 4 with 5 and 6, it appears that in those cases in which there was a woman on the panel, the rate of success was substantially higher. The proportion of all-male panels was not very large, but this difference in success rate seemed substantial enough to warrant attention. With equal pay the impact of witnesses on success rates was rather different from that in sex discrimination cases. Where witnesses were presented, complainants had a somewhat higher success rate, but this was only true when the panel had a full-time chairman. Perversely, in cases where witnesses were presented to panels with part-time chairmen, the success rate was actually lower! Looking at the relative importance of the different variables, it appears that in equal pay cases, success was highest among those complainants heard by full-time chairmen, followed by those appearing before panels which included a woman, followed (where there were full-time chairmen) by those who presented witnesses.

Notes

1 Analyses of the sort presented in this chapter are fairly unreliable when performed on small samples. Therefore, analyses of the Scottish cases are included only when the information is particularly helpful – for example, when they reflect a difference in administrative policy.

2 Schlei and Grossman (1983), provides a discussion of the fact that in courts in the United States, judicial deference to employers' use of subjective criteria increases when upper level managerial or professional promotions are involved (see Ch 17, Section IV, p.588).

3 This information is only about cases that went to a hearing. For some groups, this is offset by high rates of settlements. See Leonard (1986).

4 Because there were so few multiple-complainant cases in these years, these observations would not be true for earlier years.

5 Because the figures available on workforce size were somewhat imprecise, no attempt was made to correlate this information with case outcome.

6 The three-year figures given are for the 215 *hearings* held. The information on claims is for 148 sex discrimination *claims* and 70 equal pay *claims*.

7 See note 6.

8 COIT figures on hearings in all jurisdictions for 1980-1982 showed that about 50% were completed in less than four hours, and about 30% lasted more than four hours but finished in one day. Since the tribunal decisions themselves contain only the days the tribunal sat, it was impossible to obtain an equally precise analysis of the length of the sex discrimination and equal pay hearings.

9 In 1980 and 1981, sex discrimination and equal pay complainants with two-day hearings were far more successful (25% and 46%) than those with hearings of one day (19% and 30%). However, the reverse was true in 1982 (13% successful after two-day hearings; 37% successful after one-day hearings); and over the three-year period, success rates at one-day and two-day hearings were identical (29%).

10 Leonard (1986).

11 Leonard (1986).

CHAPTER 6

FINDINGS AND RECOMMENDATIONS

Summary of Findings

The Parties

Of the 215 tribunal hearings on sex discrimination and equal pay claims held in England and Wales during 1980-1982:
- 80% were brought by women;
- only 10% were brought by two or more complainants jointly;
- the great majority of men's claims concerned discrimination in recruitment and/or hiring for jobs; whereas the largest category of claims brought by women concerned discrimination in dismissal and selection for redundancy;
- 23% of the respondents were central or local government entities, or nationalised industries; 40% were registered companies with workforces of substantial size (at least half had 500 employees or more); only a few were companies with fewer than 20 employees.
- complainants were self-represented at more than one-third of their hearings;
- respondents had legally qualified or other specialist representatives at hearings far more frequently than complainants;
- only one-quarter of the complainants took witnesses to their hearings, with fewer than one in 12 taking more than one witness; while over half of the respondents took more than one person to testify, with over half of these presenting two, three, or more witnesses in addition to their primary witness.

Patterns and Problems in Tribunals' Decisions

Errors

The tribunal decisions revealed that, although a number of tribunals were familiar with the sex discrimination and equal pay legislation, some tribunals clearly misunderstood and/or misapplied the SDA 1975 and the EQPA 1970, or were unaware of their provisions. There were errors about the employment covered by the legislation, the types of compensation available when discrimination is proved, the relevance of a respondent's intent or motive, the concepts of indirect discrimination and 'genuine

131

occupational qualifications,' and the inappropriateness of general-ised sex-based assumptions.

The Wrong Legal Standard

Many tribunals appeared to have applied the wrong legal stan-dard: asking not 'whether the complainant was treated less favou-ably than a person of the other sex who was similarly situated,' but asking merely whether the employer's actions had been 'reason-able'.

Superficial Analysis of Employers' Explanations

Tribunals' analysis of respondents' explanations for their actions tended to be superficial. Although a number of decisions documented a careful analysis of the evidence presented, the tribunals generally, and with striking frequency, accepted vague and generalised explanations from respondents, ignored noted inconsistencies in evidence, and even accepted in proof of non-discrimination evidence which was irrelevant to the issues pre-sented.

Reliance upon Irrelevant Matters

Despite the fact that benevolent motive and good intentions are not a defence to complaints of discrimination, the tribunals frequently commented upon respondent employers' intentions, honesty, and generosity, and expressed concern with com-plainants' 'objectives' and behaviour. They appeared to rely heavily upon these matters.

Lack of Uniformity

One of the most striking characteristics in the tribunal decisions was the extent to which they reveal a lack of uniformity in tribunals' level of expertise in the legislation, the extent to which they examine respondents' explanations, and their degree of participation in the hearings. The decisions also reveal a lack of uniformity in tribunals' positions on various substantive issues, including the significance of past discrimination by a respondent; the approach to a claim of discrimination in promotion; the approach to issues of like work and material differences; the 'justifiability' of indirect discrimination; the valuation of the loss of employment opportunity and of injury to feelings; and the signifi-cance of responses to the s.74 questionnaire. These differences appeared to be related to the level of expertise of the com-plainant's representative, as well as to the expertise of the particular tribunal panel. There is enormous variation in the contents of the tribunal decisions: some provide information on the parties, the evidence, the issues raised, their findings and the reasons for them. Others provide so little information as to make it impossible to determine what act or practice was claimed to have been discriminatory and why the tribunal dismissed the claim.

Explaining the Problems

Panel Composition

Despite a stated practice of assigning to sex discrimination and equal pay hearings full-time tribunal chairmen (who are generally regarded as the more experienced), full-time chairmen presided at only two-thirds of the sex discrimination claims and only half of the equal pay claims heard in England and Wales in the period studied. In contrast, a full-time chairman was assigned to every such case in Scotland. Despite a stated objective of including a woman on each tribunal panel hearing a sex discrimination or equal pay case, in England and Wales one in 10 sex discrimination cases and one in four equal pay cases were heard by all-male panels. The worst record was in the most recent year, when one-third of equal pay cases were decided by all-male panels. In Scotland, at least one woman sat on the panel of every sex discrimination and equal pay case. Considering sex discrimination and equal pay hearings together and viewing panel composition as a whole, complainants lacked *either* a full-time chairman *or* a woman on the panel, or had *neither*, at 33% of the hearings in 1980, 40% in 1981, and 45% in 1982. Only 5% of the hearings in England and Wales were heard by a chairwoman. The choice to assign a chairwoman was almost always a choice to assign a part-time chair, as there was only one full-time chairwoman at that time. This was not the situation in Scotland, where there was a full-time chairwoman who, during the three-year period studied, was assigned to seven of the 13 hearings on claims of sex discrimination and equal pay.

Lack of Opportunity to Develop Expertise

Neither tribunal chairmen nor panel members were gaining expertise in sex discrimination and equal pay cases through experience. Cases were assigned wholly at random; therefore over the entire three-year period studied, the 215 hearings were distributed among *116 different chairmen*: only seven chairmen heard more than one case a year. The situation was even more extreme with panel members: 379 individuals were assigned to only one case each. Thus only five individuals sat on as many as one case each year. Unlike unfair dismissal cases, where both chairmen and panel members gain extensive experience fairly quickly, the assignment patterns for sex discrimination and equal pay cases appear to make it virtually impossible to expect a panel member or most chairmen to develop any meaningful expertise in the legislation through experience.

Lack of Training

During the period of this study, chairmen received no specific formal training of any kind that related to sex discrimination or equal pay issues. Panel members were given two half-day training sessions each year, though a few regions did more. These sessions sometimes dealt with equality legislation and related issues.

Confusion with Unfair Dismissal Cases

Tribunals appear to be confusing the legal standard applicable to sex discrimination cases (equal treatment) with that applicable to unfair dismissal and unfair selection for redundancy cases (reasonableness). This does not seem to be occurring in equal pay cases.

Lack of Relevant and Probative Evidence

Tribunal decisions are replete with references to failures by complainants and their representatives to present the tribunal with relevant evidence sufficient to support their claims, including failure to present necessary witnesses, failure to present statistical and comparative evidence, and failure to cross-examine respondents' witnesses effectively. These inadequacies in case development and presentation may be forcing the tribunals to rely upon more personal judgements than would be necessary if adequate evidentiary presentations were made. Many sex discrimination and equal pay complainants, and their representatives, are presenting mainly testimonial evidence to support their claims: in about half the cases studied, the parties presented testimony only, or testimony and only one or two pre-existing documents.

Perhaps not surprisingly, the success rate of claims rose directly with the amount of documentation available to the tribunal: complainants who presented testimonial evidence and a few existing documents won approximately one quarter of their claims, whereas complainants with 'specialised' evidence won approximately twice as frequently. In 1982, complainants who presented specialised evidence won 70% of their claims.

Limited Tribunal Assistance

Despite the fact that the tribunals have considerable power to direct the hearings procedure, hearings are generally regarded as adversarial in nature. In practice, tribunal chairmen and panels vary widely in the degree and nature of their participation in hearings. A few take quite active roles; many others quite clearly do not see this as appropriate. However, even those willing to intervene feel constrained by the need to retain the appearance as well as the fact of objectivity. This results in many tribunal chairmen not greatly assisting parties in presenting their cases, even where they are unrepresented.

Advice and Representation for Complainants

Case decisions reveal frequent failures by complainants to obtain timely and accurate advice on sex discrimination and equal pay claims, and a frequent failure by complainants and their representatives to develop and present necessary and relevant evidence in support of their allegations.

Failure to File Timely Applications

The three-month limit for filing sex discrimination complaints caused problems to many complainants: even after taking advice from a trade union, the EOC, or from a solicitor, a substantial number of complainants missed the deadline and their cases were accordingly dismissed.

Failure to Identify Claims

In approximately 10% of the cases heard by the tribunals, there was the possibility of additional discrimination or equal pay claims, which were neither identified by the complainant nor raised by the tribunal. In at least one-third of these cases, the complainant was represented by a trade union official or some other representative.

Failure to Identify and Present Necessary Evidence

With overwhelming frequency, complainants are failing to identify and to present at their tribunal hearings evidence sufficient to prove their claims of sex discrimination, such as necessary witnesses and comparative and statistical evidence. This is occurring when complainants are represented, as well as when they are not. These particular problems are less frequent with representatives who are legally qualified.

Job Centres

In some cases, job centre personnel had assisted complainants by correcting an employer's discriminatory actions in the first instance, by directing the complainant to the EOC, or by actually attending the tribunal hearing and testifying on the complainant's behalf. In several other cases, however, the job centre had honoured an employer's discriminatory recruiting practices, or had advised an employer that a given practice was permissible when, in fact, it was in violation of the sex discrimination legislation.

The Trades Unions

A number of tribunal decisions criticised representation by trades union officers for giving incorrect advice and for inadequate case presentation. Perhaps more important, in several cases the complainants' claims were in direct conflict with their unions: of 215 cases, five decisions indicated an entrenched and active workforce and/or union opposition to the complainant's position; and in approximately ten, the complainant's claim for equal pay or unfair selection for redundancy ran counter to a union-agreed or supported wage structure or redundancy procedure. There were also several cases where particular actions of union stewards or other officials either before or at the hearing were directly contrary to the complainant's interest. In several cases, the conflict between the complainant's claim and the union position meant the complainant was unrepresented; in others, it simply meant the representative was in the very awkward position of propounding a position that ran counter to union policy.

The Equal Opportunities Commission

The case decisions reflected a few problems encountered by those complainants who had consulted the EOC. Generally, these appeared to concern administrative and procedural matters rather than the substantive legal advice provided (e.g., problems arising from delay in obtaining advice, failure to request tribunal hearing postponements in time).

The Regional Offices of Industrial Tribunals

The few cases where the ROITs communicated with unrepresented complainants in order to obtain further information about their claims or to set deadlines for responses, revealed a marked inability in these complainants to understand and to handle such matters competently.

Explaining Complainants' Success

Certain *types of claims* were markedly more successful than others. For example, both men and women who brought claims of discrimination in recruitment and hiring won about 40% of their hearings, whereas claims of discrimination in dismissal were far less successful (less than 25% succeeded), as were claims of victimisation (10%). This suggests that success is in part a reflection of the varying degrees of difficulty encountered in the location and presentation of evidence of discrimination in the different types of cases.

Representation

Representation is unquestionably an important factor in complainant success at sex discrimination and equal pay hearings. Complainants with legal representation won considerably more often than those with trades union representation, lay representation, or self-representation. However, a more precise explanation of representatives' success is probably their level of knowledge of the equality legislation, which is complex and unique, as well as their knowledge and experience of tribunal procedure and case presentation.

Composition of the Tribunal

The presence of full-time chairmen rather than part-time chairmen, the presence of a woman on the panel, and the presentation of witnesses by the complainant all appeared to contribute to the likelihood of success for a complainant. 28% of sex discrimination claims heard by full-time chairmen were successful; while only 21% of those heard by part-time chairmen were successful. With equal pay cases, complainants heard by full-time chairmen won twice as often as those with part-time chairmen (38% vs. 19%). In equal pay cases, success rates were substantially higher where panels included a woman, both with full-time chairmen (40% rather than 25%) and with part-time chairmen (25% rather than 8%). In Scotland, where there was a full-time chairman and a woman on every panel, the success rate was 42%.

In sex discrimination cases, the presence of witnesses for the complainant corresponded with dramatic increases in success: the success rate for complainants who presented witnesses was at least twice that of those who did not, and many times greater for those whose cases were heard by part-time chairmen.

In equal pay cases, there was a slight increase in success in those cases where complainants presented witnesses (29% to 33%).

Conclusions and Recommendations

There are primarily two factors preventing the proper adjudication of sex discrimination and equal pay claims in the industrial tribunals. One is a situation within the tribunals themselves: many of the tribunal chairmen and panel members who are hearing the cases lack adequate expertise in the equality legislation. This situation is explainable, even understandable, but it is no less damaging for that. The other problem is inadequate fact development and presentation of complainants' cases, which occurs frequently both with unrepresented complainants and with certain types of representatives. The advice and representation complainants are receiving is, at best, uneven, and, too frequently, it is disastrously inaccurate.

Below we outline some possibilities for ameliorating these problems, including a few legislative changes. Separately, we discuss the significance of our findings with regard to three proposals for more basic change which are currently being debated: changing the burden of proof, creating specialised tribunals to hear equal rights cases, and adopting an inquisitorial approach rather than the adversarial process currently in use.

During the last several years, recommendations for changes in handling sex discrimination and equal pay claims in the tribunal system have been proposed by interested groups and individuals, including the EOC and the NCCL. Others, such as the CRE and the EOC for Northern Ireland, have made recommendations in their own areas which are related and useful. Some of these groups' comments are noted in the discussion below, but a review of their proposals in their entirety is recommended to the interested reader.[1]

Increasing Tribunal Expertise

The crucial finding of this study with respect to the tribunals themselves is that even several years into the equality legislation, many tribunals were making errors both about specific provisions of the SDA 1975 and the EQPA, and in the way they were analysing evidence in cases before them. These errors were directly affecting complainants' success and were leading to inconsistent decisions among tribunals. Because the number of such cases heard is small, the random system of assignment used meant few chairmen or panel members heard more than one such case in a year, a number insufficient to develop expertise through experience; and at the time of this study, neither group was receiving any formal training in the legislation.

If errors and inconsistencies in tribunal decisions are to decrease, it is essential to raise the level of expertise in the equality legislation in those tribunal panels which hear discrimination and equal pay claims. Our findings suggest several steps which would help achieve this:

Full-time Chair

A full-time chair should be assigned to every case which includes a sex discrimination or equal pay claim.

Women Panel Members

There should be a woman on the panel for every sex discrimination or equal pay case.

Training

Chairs and panel members assigned to sex discrimination and equal pay cases should receive training and re-training in the provisions of the SDA 1975 and the EQPA 1970, and in the case law which defines the appropriate method of analysing cases brought under these Acts.

Case Assignment

Tribunals should adopt a case assignment procedure which develops expertise in at least a few chairs and panel members. The present system of random assignments does not permit chairs and members to develop expertise through experience; rather, it assures that many will have only limited experience.

Designated Duty Chairs and Members

Each region should designate two full-time chairs and a certain group of panel members who would hear all claims of sex discrimination and equal pay for a given period, perhaps two or three years. Such a system, using designated 'duty chairs', is followed in racial discrimination cases brought before the county courts. In addition to helping increase expertise, this system would be economical, since training could be tailored to the smaller group regularly handling the cases. It would also reduce some of the problems administrators presently encounter in assigning and scheduling sex discrimination and equal pay cases, the length of which is found to be more difficult to predict than that of cases concerning unfair dismissal.

Guidelines on Recurring Issues

Guidelines could be developed for the panels on the recurring issues in sex discrimination and equal pay cases. The tribunals now have detailed guidelines on the issue of dismissal for various reasons (illness, incompetence, criminal offences, absenteeism, redundancy, etc.); a similar guide could be provided for equality cases.

Amicus Curiae Briefs

The EOC could be allowed to submit *amicus curiae* briefs in cases where they were not involved as representatives or parties. These are briefs on the law applicable to the particular case before a tribunal, filed not as a party to the case, but as a 'friend of the tribunal' for its assistance addressing the issues presented.

Improving Advice and Representation

The other urgent need identified by this study is for knowledgeable advice and representation for individuals who believe they have a sex discrimination or equal pay claim. At present, the lack of such assistance results in a significant number of complainants failing to file their cases within the required deadlines, and in an even larger number making seriously deficient submissions to the tribunals. The magnitude of this problem justifies a major effort on the part of all agencies and individuals who are or might be in a position to assist complainants, to consider carefully the steps that could be taken directly or indirectly to improve the situation. It is to be hoped that the EOC as the agency with special responsibility and expertise in this areas, would take a significant supportive role in this. A few possibilities can be noted:

Advice

Job centres, CABX, law centres, and the trades unions must be better informed. The EOC already has materials and expertise which it could provide to these and other interested groups.Certainly the EOC has publications which could be of great assistance if they were widely distributed. One example is its *Casebook*, which summarises the provisions of both Acts and all the major tribunal and higher court decisions on sex discrimination and equal pay cases. This could be an important help to advice centres, to advocacy groups, and to other representatives as well, but it is relatively little known. Wider distribution of the *Casebook*, perhaps free of charge, might in itself be of considerable influence and assistance.

The EOC has staff well qualified to instruct others on the legislation. If, in view of its static budget, the EOC is unable to undertake such efforts with its own staff, it could provide limited aid to individuals or groups who could assume that responsibility and/or it could actively lend its support to fund raising efforts to finance such activity from other sources.

Representation

With respect to representation, one obvious possibility is for the EOC to provide support for more cases itself. Whether or not this is a realistic possibility, the EOC should attempt to encourage and assist the development of expert representatives on a far more widespread level than currently exists. A training packet could be sent to any solicitor or barrister who indicated a willingness to take such cases. Law centres could, in a variety of ways, be urged to develop expertise in equal rights issues. Perhaps in areas of the country where cases are most frequent, special efforts could be undertaken to assist the development of expertise in existing community agencies. Finally, should legal aid be extended to tribunal hearings, the Commission could supply a briefing packet to any solicitor or barrister who took up sex discrimination or equal pay cases.

The Trades Unions

It is worth noting separately that, with respect to both advice and representation, the unevenness of trades unions' expertise in and support for sex discrimination and equal pay claims seems so critical a problem that a special initiative in that direction would be warranted.

Changes in Statutory Provisions

A number of changes in statutory provisions would be of certain assistance both in increasing tribunal expertise and in minimising the effect of the lack of informed advice available to individuals.

Filing Time Limit

The three-month time limit for filing sex discrimination claims is the shortest period for filing such a claim in the countries of the European Community.[2] It has been a major obstacle to individuals pursuing legitimate sex discrimination claims. The lack of know-ledgeable advice in many advisory agencies and in the trades unions exacerbates its effect, as delay in obtaining correct information is frequent. In 1980, the EOC recommended that the period within which proceedings must be brought be extended from three to five months.[3] While this would be a step in the right direction, it would not be enough to eliminate the problem which exists. The time limit should be extended to five or even six months for all complainants with sex discrimination claims.

EOC Right to Initiate Proceedings

To encourage greater use of the EOC's considerable and unique expertise, the EOC should be permitted to initiate tribunal proceedings in its own name.[4]

Class Action

At present individuals may, with the permission of the tribunal or by agreement with the respondent, bring joint claims, but this is no longer frequently done. A formal mechanism for joint claims such as the class action permitted in the United States, would permit complainants with similar claims to consolidate them into a single action. This would be likely to encourage greater attention to the development and submission of relevant evidence by the parties, and to encourage greater acceptance by the tribunals of a broader range of evidence.[5]

Power to Refer Cases to a Higher Forum

It would also be useful for the industrial tribunals to have the same power in sex discrimination and equal pay cases as the county courts were given by the Supreme Courts Act 1981: to refer cases to a higher court when the tribunal itself considers it advisable because of the complexity of the factual or legal issues.

Current Debates on Other Possible Changes

Three major proposals concerning more basic changes are currently being discussed by experts and commentators as follows:
(1) changing the burden of proof;
(2) creating a specialised discrimination tribunal; and
(3) adopting a more inquisitorial approach in tribunal proceedings.
The relevance of this study to these proposals is examined below.

The Burden of Proof

The EOC[6] and the NCCL[7] have both recommended that the burden of proof in sex discrimination cases be shifted to the respondent after the complainant has shown that they have been treated less favourably than a person of the opposite sex was or would have been treated in the same circumstances. This shift would require the employer then to satisfy the tribunal by a preponderance of the evidence that discrimination had *not* occurred. Groups in Greece, the Netherlands, and the Federal Republic of Germany have made similar recommendations to their governments.[8] It is thought appropriate to place a substantial burden on the party with the easier access to or control of the relevant evidence, which in sex discrimination cases, is usually the employer.

A number of English lawyers experienced in discrimination law have expressed the view that if there were a heavier burden upon the respondent, tribunals would tend to require more in the way of explanation from employers than they currently do. They have generally supported the procedure followed in courts in the United

States, whereby after the complainant establishes a *prima facie* case, the burden passes to the employer to produce evidence that they acted for a legitimate, non-discriminatory reason. Bindman, noting the tendency of tribunals to accept an employer's uncorroborated claim that race 'was not in his mind' as a full explanation of actions which were *prima facie* discriminatory, has explained:

> Once the applicant had established less favourable treatment than that received by one from another social group (or sex) the burden of proof now shifted to the respondent should be a heavier one. It should not be enough for him merely to show a plausible alternative ground and thereby shift the burden back to the applicant to show that race was the more probable ground. The respondent should retain the burden of proving that his explanation was the more probable.[9]

In 1981 the EAT expressed its scepticism about the usefulness of this 'shift in the evidential burden.' In *Khanna v Ministry of Defence* [1981] IRLR 331 it said:

> . . . we think Industrial Tribunals may find it easier to forget about the rather nebulous concept of the 'shift in the evidential burden.' . . . in our view it is more likely to obscure than to illuminate the right answer . . . The right course in this case was for the Industrial Tribunal to take into account the fact that direct evidence of discrimination is seldom going to be available and that, accordingly, in these cases the affirmative evidence of discrimination will normally consist of inferences to be drawn from the primary facts. If the primary facts indicate that there has been discrimination of some kind, the employer is called on to give an explanation and, failing clear and specific explanation being given by the employer to the satisfaction of the Industrial Tribunal, an inference of unlawful discrimination from the primary facts will mean the complaint succeeds. . . .

Since *Khanna*, however, commentators have remarked that the EAT's own formula involves several concepts which are in themselves both vague and difficult. For example, Donnelly calls for at least more guidance from the EAT and higher courts on these matters:

> Although the case of *Khanna v Ministry of Defence* gives some guidance to tribunals on the difficult problem of the burden of proof, it does not lay down in any way what

industrial tribunals are to look for in deciding whether a *prima facie* case has been established. Nor has any guidance been given on what evidence they may consider acceptable from a respondent to justify his actions. That is not to say that the superior courts should lay down in minute detail the countless variations which may establish a *prima facie* case or the myriad of reasons which could constitute a valid non-discriminatory explanation for the alleged discrimination, but guidelines which set the broad parameters of the complainant's and the respondent's cases would, it is submitted, be of great assistance to tribunals. In addition, guidance from the superior courts on the dangers of accepting the subjective assessment of their own actions by the alleged discriminators, in the absence of objective evidence, would also be of assistance.[10]

Pannick contends that the EAT's remarks simply mask difficulties which will remain, and continues to advocate the procedure which places a heavier burden of proof on the employer. He argues:

> The application of this theory of burden of proof to discrimination actions would give the tribunals a principled framework for the resolution of the difficulties of proof which the British courts have hitherto treated in an ad hoc manner and which have limited the use of the 1975 and 1976 Acts.[11]

This study has shown that tribunals very often accept explanations from employers which appear far less than 'clear and specific'. There is little question that a heavier burden of justification upon the employer in sex discrimination cases would encourage the tribunals to be more demanding of employers and more sceptical of uncorroborated explanation of their actions. Yet other findings of the study suggest that changing the statutory burden of proof would have only minimal effect upon the outcome of sex discrimination claims unless other changes were made as well.

If a change in the burden of proof were to be meaningfully implemented the tribunals would have to become far more expert in the legislation than is presently the case. If tribunals continue mistakenly to believe the standard for cases is a 'reasonable' managerial decision, or if they continue to accord undue deference to employers' explanations, a shift in the burden of proof will change little. After all, in unfair dismissal cases the burden of proof has in the past been upon the employer, yet it is precisely these cases in which commentators feel that great deference is given to the employer!

144

Further, a change in the burden of proof would need to be put to the tribunals in sufficiently specific terms for the fact to be absorbed and put into practice. Chairmen have already stated that they would like more detailed guidance on how much evidence will establish a *prima facie* case, on what will constitute a 'clear and specific' explanation from an employer, and on how much evidence is necessary to support an inference that the reason for discriminatory treatment was the complainant's sex. Should the burden of proof change, guidance on its application would be essential.

Finally, a change in the burden of proof cannot in itself eliminate the problems of poor representation. Where a complainant presents evidence which falls short of even establishing a *prima facie* case that discrimination has occurred, and where the tribunal will not or cannot compensate for this by intervening in questioning and cross-examining, the question of a shift in the burden of poof will not even be reached.

A Special Discrimination Division in the Tribunals

Commentators and advocacy groups in the United Kingdom have suggested the use of specialist tribunal panels to handle sex discrimination and equal pay cases. The EOC for Northern Ireland, for example, has recommended the formation of a special division within their industrial tribunals, which would consist of one or two chairmen and a small number of panel members, with sole responsibility for all sex discrimination and equal pay cases.[12] In England, the CRE proposes the creation of a special division within the tribunals to hear *all* claims of both race and sex discrimination, including claims about goods, facilities, and services, which are currently heard by the county courts.[13] The NCCL and others have recommended a separate set of tribunals be established to deal with all cases of racial and sex discrimination, whether in the employment field or elsewhere.[14] A specific judgement about the relative merits of these different suggestions is beyond the scope of this study. They nevertheless have in common the primary objective of developing greater specialisation in equal rights cases, and in this they accord with several of our findings which suggest specialisation in some form is essential in order to assure an adequate level of expertise. Discrimination and equal pay cases are now so few in number that specialisation of some sort will be necessary to permit even a small number of chairmen and panel members to develop expertise through experience; especially because in these areas tribunals cannot normally rely upon expertise being supplied by the parties, even where they are represented.

This study also identifies certain clear practical advantages to be gained from specialisation. Case assignments and scheduling of both tribunal panels and the parties would be easier, and the scale of any training would be substantially reduced, since it would be required for dramatically fewer than all the possible chairmen and members who might be assigned such cases in a non-specialised system. In fact, the research highlights a danger in failing to begin specialisation. It shows that many of the errors in sex discrimination cases arise from confusion with the unfair dismissal and redundancy legislation. Moreover, it determines that one-third of all claims of sex discrimination concern dismissal or redundancy, and that many of them are joined with specific claims under the Employment Protection (Consolidation) Act.[15] It must be assumed therefore, that the possibilities for confusion and error will continue to exist in a large proportion of sex discrimination cases if the system continues without specialisation.

There would, however, be benefits from specialisation beyond the mere administrative convenience and the elimination of blatant error in tribunal decisions. With the development of expertise, panels would be able to give more assistance to parties. Decisions would be better informed, even where the tribunal did not have the benefit of knowledgeable representatives. Ultimately this would result in greater consistency among decisons, a matter of no little importance to complainants and to respondents both in accepting the outcome of their own particular conflicts and in their ability accurately to predict the consequences of policies and practices in employment matters in general.

Modification of the Adversarial Model

At present the industrial tribunals operate on an adversarial model: it is considered the sole responsibility of the parties themselves to produce the evidence necessary to prove their case. As discussed in Chapter 3, there are among chairmen and panel members those who participate in the hearings more actively than others, with those in Scotland appearing to participate more actively than those elsewhere. But the general feeling nonetheless is that such participation *must* be limited to maintain the tribunal's appearance of impartiality. Moreover, as noted, except in the simplest of cases, it cannot possibly be expected that intervention by the tribunal for the first time at the hearing can provide assistance in the crucial task of identifying and obtaining necessary evidence and witnesses.

Some commentators advocate more participation by the tribunal panels, urging them to take a more 'investigative' approach.

The EOC for Northern Ireland has formally recommended this approach for tribunals dealing with sex discrimination and equal pay cases there. It has said:

> Where an applicant is unrepresented, the chairman should be ready to intervene to ensure that all the appropriate issues of fact and law are properly aired. Even where an applicant *is* represented – be it by a lay person or a legal practitioner – the chairman should not permit any matters of either fact or law to be less than fully examined.[16]

A more substantial change is recommended by two British lawyers who have recently completed a comparative analysis of the provisions for legal redress for discriminatory treatment in the various countries of the EEC, about half of which have inquisitorial systems for hearing sex discrimination and equal pay claims. They conclude that the tribunals or courts which deal with such cases should be inquisitorial rather than adversarial in nature. The scheme recommended would include the active direction of procedure by chairmen (or judges) familiar with and well-versed in law. It would, however, also include a court official such as the French 'rapporteur',[17] an individual expert in the legislation who in each case reviews the available information, determines which evidence and witnesses would be appropriate, and ensures that they are produced by the parties. The research in this study is a useful source for consideration of these suggestions. It documents the lack of knowledgeable advice and representation available to complainants, a factor clearly limiting their chances of successfully proving their sex discrimination and equal pay claims in the existing adversarial system. Knowledgeable assistance from some source is clearly essential, and this could certainly include assistance from within the tribunal system itself.

The more interventionist approach in Scotland suggests much more could be done even within roughly the same rules of procedure. Indeed, there are tribunal chairmen who believe that far more active direction of cases could be achieved with the present tribunal rules of procedure in England, with tribunals holding pre-hearing assessments of evidence, scheduling the discovery of documents, etc. Interviews with complainants suggest that parties would not find more intervention objectionable – some would actually welcome it – where it was managed in an even-handed manner. The major limitation upon this idea (and it is a serious one) is that for fact development to be effective it must begin early in a case; and it must be informal. It is difficult to imagine that an unrepresented complainant could regard a pre-hearing assessment before a tribunal chairman as the occasion for a free and open discussion of their complaint, to determine what they need to begin to do to collect their evidence. This, it can be assumed, is why the authors of the comparative analysis conclude that, in addition to an expert and involved chairman, there is need for a specialist devoted to the particular task of fact development.

This suggestion deserves thoughtful consideration in view of the widespread and serious need for assistance for complainants documented in this study. The model it envisages certainly has significant advantages. It would stream-line the processing of cases, both by minimising the need for the participation of a full tribunal panel on preliminary matters, and by eliminating the occasions when hearings must be adjourned to allow one party or both to gather additional evidence. Confronting the parties with an expert at the outset should lead to the early identification of frivolous claims or defences and, in exploring the strengths of claims, should encourage appropriate settlements. Perhaps most important, it would assure that bona fide claims of substance – rather than succumbing to misinformation, minor technicalities, or even error on the part of tribunals and representatives – would proceed to judgement on the merits by expert, fully-informed tribunals.

Notes

1   A summary of the changes recommended by the EOC appears in its 1980 *Annual Report*, at p39 and in *Legislating for Change*, EOC 1986. Recommendations from the NCCL are discussed in Scorer and Sedley (1983). A discussion of some of the issues and possibilities can be found in Hepple (1983), pp71, 90. Two other publications are useful and quite relevant: EOC for Northern Ireland 1981, and CRE 1985.

2   Corcoran and Donnelly (1984).

3   EOC *Annual Report*, 1980.

4   Pannick, (1985), p283, points out that the original reason for depriving the EOC of such power was that it had the power to bring a formal investigation. In view of the lack of effective power in an informal investigation, he argues this original reason is no longer valid.

5   On the other hand, the American experience indicates that class actions present considerable practical and procedural difficulties. Pannick (1975), pp284-301, summarises the advantages and difficulties of adapting the class action to the British legal system. Certainly this procedure would not be likely to be used frequently, and it should at best be regarded as only one means among many to eliminate the problems identified in this study.

6   EOC *Annual Report*, 1980.

7   Scorer and Sedley (1983).

8   Corcoran and Donnelly (1984), p55.

9   Bindman 1980 (LSG 77:46).
10   Donnelly (1982). The author was formerly Deputy Legal Advisor to the EOC.
11   Pannick (1981).
12   EOC for Northern Ireland, 1981.
13   CRE, 1985.
14   Scorer and Sedley (1983). For a discussion of other proposals, see Hepple (1983), pp71-90.
15   Leonard (1986).
16   EOC for Northern Ireland, 1981, p19.
17   Corcoran and Donnelly (1984), pp79, 46.

APPENDIX 1

TRENDS IN REPRESENTATION AT SEX DISCRIMINATION AND EQUAL PAY HEARINGS 1976-1982

As noted in the text, these DE statistics present information for each *complainant*, rather than for each *case*. In years when there were many multiple-complainant cases, this will change any comparative figures substantially. Although the statistics themselves provide no information on the frequency of multiple-complainant cases or the number of complainants they included, our detailed review of files at COIT suggested they were most frequent in equal pay cases in the years 1976-1978.

Representation in the multiple-complainant cases (especially the equal pay cases) was often by the complainants' trade union. This means two things in terms of interpreting the statistics. First, the number of tribunal hearings handled by trades unions is likely to be far lower than the number of individual complainants represented by them. For example, the 521 individuals who filed equal pay claims in 1976 and had trades union representation may well have consititited only 50 cases. If that were so, it would mean that although 521/797 or 65% of the complainants had trades union representation, in terms of actual hearings held, there would have been trades union representation at only 50 of 326, or 15%. Secondly, since most multiple-complainant cases were handled by the unions, the numbers of *individuals* with other types of representation (or no representation) are probably fairly close to the number of actual *hearings*.

Table 1 Complainants' type of representation at SDA hearings, 1976-1983

Type of representative	1976		1977		1978		1979		1980		1981		1982		1983		TOTAL	
	No	%	No	%	No	%	No	%	No	%	No	%	No	%	No	%	No	%
Solicitor/Counsel*	9	4	11	14	20	30	18	29	22	29	34	38	18	32	60	53	192	27
Trade union*	91	52	20	26	12	18	7	11	12	16	16	18	9	16	12	11	179	25
Self	52	30	32	42	23	34	19	31	29	38	31	34	21	37	20	18	227	32
Other	10	6	4	5	7	10	12	20	10	13	7	8	8	14	21	18	79	11
Rep not present	4	2	5	7	1	1	2	3	3	4	0	–	0	–	0	–	15	2
Type rep unknown	8	5	4	5	4	6	3	5	1	1	2	2	0	–	0	–	22	3
Total	174		76		67		61		77		90		56		113		714	

Source: DE Statistics, Table 2(6).

* There is no clear rule for classifying solicitors who are employed by trades unions; they may have been placed in either of the categories indicated.

Table 2 Complainants' type of representation at EQPA hearings, 1976-1983†

Type of representative	1976		1977		1978		1979		1980		1981		1982		1983		TOTAL	
	No	%	No	%	No	%	No	%	No	%	No	%	No	%	No	%	No	%
Solicitor/Counsel*	34	4	67	16	35	30	6	8	5	19	10	33	6	43	4	44	167	11
Trade union*	521	65	247	58	55	47	58	73	4	15	4	13	2	14	2	22	893	59
Self	156	20	87	20	12	10	10	13	13	50	9	30	5	36	3	33	295	20
Other	59	7	10	2	10	8	1	1	3	11	5	17	1	7	0	–	89	6
Rep not present	2	0	3	1	0	–	1	1	0	–	1	3	0	–	0	–	7	–
Type rep unknown	25	3	12	3	6	5	3	4	1	4	1	3	0	–	0	–	48	3
Total	797		426		118		79		26		30		14		9		1499	

Source: DE Statistics, Table 10(6).

† As Chapter 1 indicates, 2,147 individuals had hearings on EQPA applications in these eight years. To decrease the distortion caused by cases of one extremely large multiple-complainant case in 1980 in which the type of representation was unknown, that case is here counted as one case only, as it involved only a single tribunal proceeding.

Some percentage totals do not add up to exactly 100% because of rounding of numbers.

* There is no clear rule for classifying solicitors who are employed by trades unions; they may have been placed in either of the categories indicated.

APPENDIX 2

COMPLAINANTS' REPRESENTATION

Table 1 *Complainants' type of representation at SDA hearings,*
1980-1982

	1980 77 hearings† %	1981 90 hearings %	1982 56 hearings %	Total 223 hearings %
Solicitor/Counsel*	29	38	32	34
Trade union*	16	18	16	17
Self	38	34	37	36
Other	13	8	14	11
Rep not present	4	–	–	1
Type rep unknown	1	2	–	1

Source: DE Statistics Table 2(G).

Table 2 *Complainants' type of representation at EQPA hearings,*
1980-1982

	1980 26 hearings %	1981 30 hearings %	1982 14 hearings %	Total 70 hearings %
Solicitor/Counsel*	19	33	43	30
Trade union*	15	13	14	14
Self	50	30	36	39
Other	11	17	7	13
Rep not present	–	3	–	1
Type rep unknown	4††	3	–	3

Source: DE Statistics, Table 10(G).

*There is no clear rule for classifying solicitors who are employed by trades unions; they may have been placed in either of the categories indicated.
† The original DE figures for 1980 showed only 68 hearings held. But a recent revised count by the DE shows 77 hearings. This information and the revised figures were provided by the DE.

†† These figures on complainants' representation 1980-1982 include a 649-complainant case in 1980, for which the type of representative is listed as 'unknown.' It is more accurate to view these as a single case, since it was actually handled that way, and only one representative would have been involved. Table 3 shows the numbers for 1980, both 'raw' and 'adjusted'.

Table 3   *Complainants' type of representation at EQPA hearings in 1980, adjusted and unadjusted figures*

Type of representative	1980 Unadjusted		1980 Adjusted	
	No	%	No	%
Solicitor/Counsel*	5	.8	5	19.2
Trade union*	4	.6	4	15.4
Self	13	1.9	13	50
Other	3	.5	3	11.5
Rep not present	0	–	0	
Type rep unknown	649	96.3	1	3.8
Total	674	100	26	100

Source: DE Statistics, Tables 10(G).

CASE CITATIONS

Chapter 2

Chapter 3

Chapter 4

BIBLIOGRAPHY
Books

Dickens, L; Jones, M; Weekes, B; and Hart, M, *Dismissed* (Basil Blackwell, Oxford, 1985).

Coote, Anna; and Gill, Tess, *Women's Rights: A Practical Guide* (3rd ed), (Penguin Books, Harmondsworth, 1983).

Coussins, Jean, *The Equality Report . . . one year of the Equal Pay Act, the Sex Discrimination Act, the Equal Opportunities Commission* (NCCL, London, 1976).

Europe's 10,000 Largest Companies (Dun and Bradstreet, London, 1983).

Goodman, M J, *Industrial Tribunals Procedure* (2nd ed), (Oyez, London, 1979).

Key British Enterprises: the top 20,000 British Companies (Dun and Bradstreet, London, 1983).

Lustgarten, Laurence, *Legal Control of Racial Discrimination* (Macmillan, London, 1980).

Pannick, David, *Sex Discrimination Law* (Clarendon Press, 1985).

Schlei, B; and Grossman, P., *Employment Discrimination Law* (2nd ed), (Bureau of National Affairs, Washington, D.C., 1983).

Scorer, Catherine ; and Sedley, Ann, *Amending the Equality Laws* (NCCL, London, 1983).

Whitesides, K; and Hawker, G, *Industrial Tribunals* (Sweet and Maxwell, London, 1975).

Zander, Michael, *Cases and Materials on the English Legal System* (3rd ed), (Weidenfeld and Nicolson, London, 1982).

Periodicals

Bindman, Geoffrey, 'Proving discrimination: the importance of discovery' (1980), *Guardian Gazette* Vol 77 No 12 (The Law Society, London).

Bindman, Geoffrey, 'Proving discrimination: is the burden too heavy?' (1980), *Guardian Gazette* Vol 77 No 46 (The Law Society, London).

Bowers, John; and Clarke, Andrew, 'Unfair dismissal and managerial prerogative: a study of "other substantial reason"' (1981), *Industrial Law Journal* Vol 10 (Sweet and Maxwell, London).

Byrne, P; and Lovenduski, J, 'The Equal Opportunities Commission' (1978), *Women's Studies International* Vol 1 (Oxford).

Byrne, P; and Lovenduski, J, 'Sex equality and the law in Britain' (1978), *British Journal of Law and Society* Vol 5 No 2 (Oxford).

Collins, Hugh, 'Capitalist discipline and corporatist law' (1982-83), parts 1 and 2 *Industrial Law Journal* Vols 11 and 12 (Sweet and Maxwell, London).

Dickens, Linda, 'Do lay members influence tribunal decisions?' (November 1983), *Personnel Management* (Personnel Publications, London).

Elias, Patrick, 'Fairness in unfair dismissal: trends and tensions' (1981), *Industrial Law Journal* Vol 10 (Sweet and Maxwell, London).

Gregory, Jeanne, 'Equal pay and sex discrimination: why women are giving up the fight' (February 1982), *Feminist Review* No 10 (London).

Hawkes W R; and Smith, Gillian, 'Patterns of representation of the parties in unfair dismissal cases: a review of the evidence' (April 1981), *Department of Employment Research Paper* No 22 (London).

Hepple, B A, 'Judging equal rights' (1983), *Current Legal Problems* (Stevens, London).

Lustgarten, Laurence, 'Problems of proof in employment discrimination cases' (1977), *Industrial Law Journal* Vol 6 (Sweet and Maxwell, London).

Pannick, David, 'The burden of proof in discrimination cases' (1981), *New Law Journal* Vol 131 No 6016 (London).

Reports

Corcoran, Jennifer; and Donnelly, Elaine, *'Report of a comparative analysis of the provisions for legal redress in member states of the European Economic Community in respect of Article 119 of the Treaty of Rome and the Equal Pay, Equal Treatment and Social Security Directives'* (February 1984).

Commission for Racial Equality, *Industrial Tribunal Applicants under the Race Relations Act* (CRE, London, 1976).

Commission for Racial Equality, *Review of the Race Relations Act 1976; Proposals for Change* (CRE, London, July 1985).

Dickens, Linda; and Jones, Michael, *Statutory Protection against Unfair Dismissal in Great Britain,* (SSRC Industrial Relation Unit, University of Warwick. Paper presented in Wissenschaftszentrum, Berlin, November 1981).

Donnelly, Elaine, *The impact of the Rules of Procedure and Evidence upon Discrimination Cases before the Industrial Tribunals in England and Wales, with special reference to claims alleging Sex Discrimination,* (1982) (unpublished).

Equal Opportunities Commission for Northern Ireland, *The Industrial Tribunal System – Recommendations for Change,* (EOC for Northern Ireland, Belfast, February 1981).

HMSO, CMND. 5724, *Equality for Women,* 1974.

NCCL Women's Rights Unit, *Comments on the Government's Proposals for an Anti-Discrimination Law,* (NCCL, London, November 1973).

Graham, Cosmo; and Lewis, Norman, *The role of ACAS conciliation in Equal Pay and Sex Discrimination Cases,* (EOC, Manchester, 1985).

Leonard, Alice M, *Pyrrhic Victories: Winning Sex Discrimination and Equal Pay Cases in the Industrial Tribunals,* (HMSO, London, April 1987).

Leonard, Alice M, *The first eight years: a profile of applicants to the Industrial Tribunals under the Sex Discrimination Act 1975 and Equal Pay Act 1970,* (EOC, Manchester, 1986).